"To echo Nelson Mandela, 'Education is the most powerful weapon which you can use to change the world.' Sanjeev was a teacher that changed the way students imagined the world in them and them in the world. He inspired us not just to be better designers but also to be the best version of ourselves. He held our hand, extended his mentorship beyond the classroom, and inspired us by setting examples through his exemplary work. Thank you, Sanjeev, for believing in us and your unwavering commitment to creating possibilities."

Swati Sharma, *former student, Batch 2001, Indian Institute of Crafts and Design, Jaipur, India*

Design Education in India

This book traces developments in design education in India and shows the continuing impact of the Bauhaus School of design education, which formed the basis of the National Institute of Design. It presents the findings of the author's research and experiential learning as a design educator over a 25-year period.

This book argues that as the effects of climate change and the exploitation of natural and human resources become more pervasive, it has become increasingly important to ensure that the values of social responsibility are instilled into the design students who will become future practitioners. This book offers an alternative model of understanding regarding the ecosystem of design and sustainable design education. Going beyond description and analysis, it includes three case studies of adoptable design curricula created by the author, with student responses to the programmes to provide first-hand insights into their impact. Research findings are based on detailed interviews with contemporary faculty members, all experts in the various design disciplines, along with an in-depth survey of existing design programmes in India.

Design Education in India encourages a paradigm shift in thinking about the environment, spaces and places. It offers a unique perspective on the status of design education in an important and fast-growing economy and will be a useful read for design educators and researchers in varied disciplines.

Sanjeev Bothra (1968–2021), an alumnus of a five-year design course at the National Institute of Design (NID), Ahmedabad, India, did a year-long experiment of 'unlearning consumerist perspectives' so acquired, by spending time in rural India. Thereafter he was engaged with design education across numerous design schools and departments in and outside of India. In addition to being an educator and researcher, Sanjeev was a passionate freelance graphic designer. He was committed to the ultimate values of humanity, concern for environment and the future of the planet. This book is a culmination of his 25 years of professional practice, alongside part-time research and teaching.

Routledge Research in Social Design

Socially responsible design considers the broader environmental, economic, cultural, and political impacts of design on society. This series brings together cross-disciplinary research from a wide range of academics and design practitioners tracing the development of social design, its theoretical underpinnings and future trends. It welcomes contributions from established and early-career researchers examining social design through the lens of architecture, housing, product design and innovation, healthcare, education, cultural studies, sustainability, business, and design management.

Collaborative Social Design with Mexican Indigenous Communities
Critical Craft and Transformative Practices
Carmen Malvar

Design Education in India
Values of Socially Responsible Design
Sanjeev Bothra

For further information about this series, please visit: www.routledge.com/Routledge-Research-in-Social-Design/book-series/RRSOCDES

Design Education in India

Values of Socially Responsible Design

Sanjeev Bothra

Edited by Nita Mukherjee

First published 2024
by Routledge
4 Park Square, Milton Park, Abingdon, Oxon OX14 4RN

and by Routledge
605 Third Avenue, New York, NY 10158

Routledge is an imprint of the Taylor & Francis Group, an informa business

British Library Cataloguing-in-Publication Data
A catalogue record for this book is available from the British Library

ISBN: 978-1-032-46799-3 (hbk)
ISBN: 978-1-032-46802-0 (pbk)
ISBN: 978-1-003-38335-2 (ebk)

DOI: 10.4324/9781003383352

Typeset in Times New Roman
by codeMantra

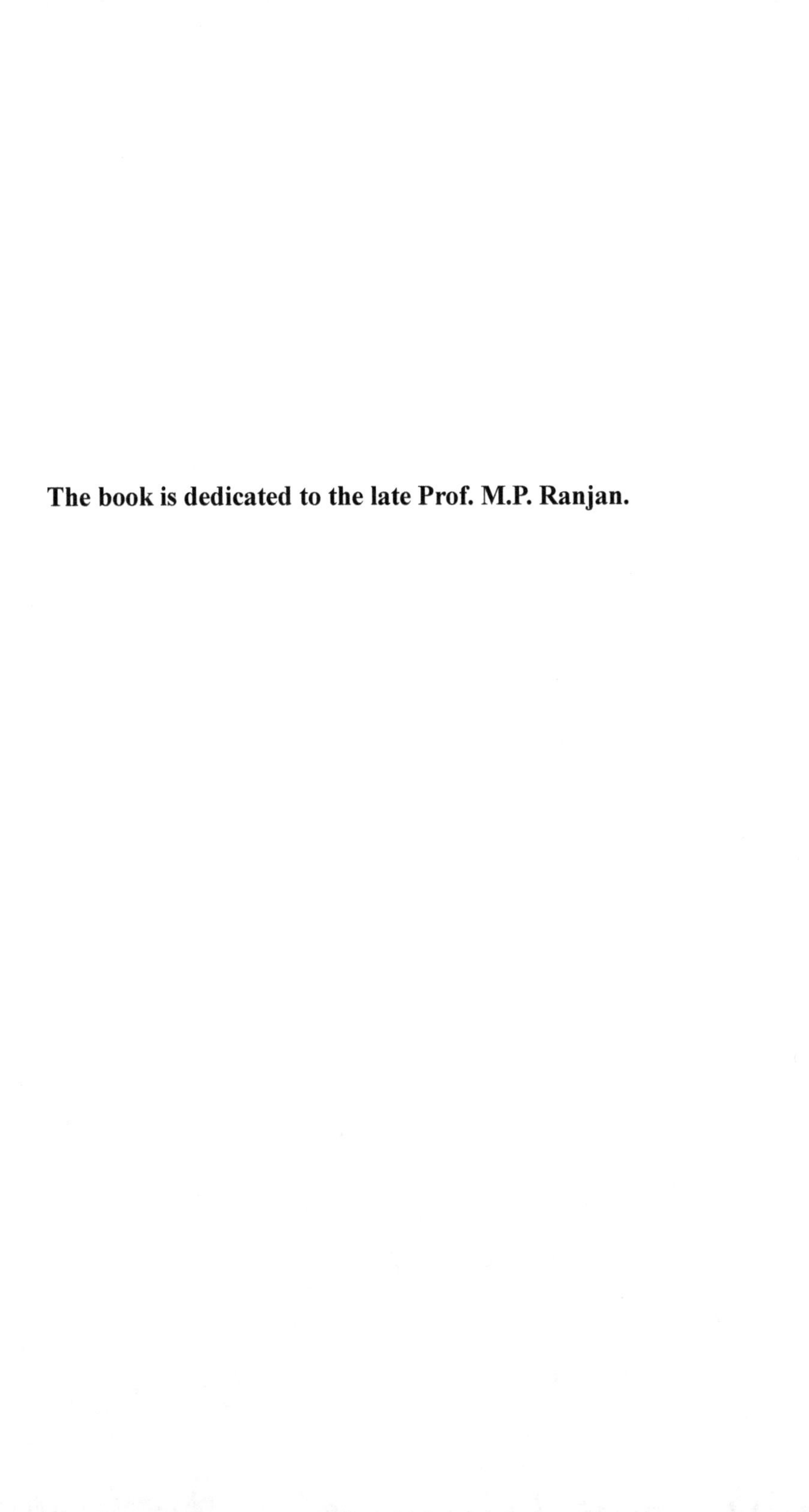

The book is dedicated to the late Prof. M.P. Ranjan.

Contents

Foreword

Sanjeev Bothra

The Design profession, like other activities, prepares and throws in several typologies of professionals. Our social context and the needs of the polity shape the characteristics of practice, the practitioners and the ideologues. All of them together shape the pedagogy that trains and shape professionals.

Design Thinking! A methodology that has gripped the imagination and gained much currency in the past two decades of this century, albeit with other professionals. The corporate world has happily borrowed, comprehended, imbibed and applied this thinking toolbox. It has helped understand the processes that underlie innovative ideas, creative story-telling and experiential products and services that have been created. Start-ups of democratised services and innovative digital products using the magic of IoT have helped transform the visibility of design and designers. The 'designerly' ability to 'connect new dots' to see newer patterns and images has gained traction.

In such a space, has emerged this thesis from the late Sanjeev Bothra, a trusted friend, a scrupulous colleague and a former student—more of the first and less of the last. This book is the story of his design and life journey. On first read, it seems an uncharted journey, where Sanjeev, the traveller, has let events, experiences and experiments define his philosophical and ideological sub-text. But as I read on and within, I seem to understand that this journey has a clear charter. The most significant commandment learnt at NID—the means and the process are more significant than the end, and the sum of parts is greater than the whole!

In the finite world we live in, with depleting resources and unscrupulous gain-seeking, 'design thinking' needs a realignment, a re-purposing. This thesis turned book of Sanjeev's, moves towards this 'design rethink', hopefully moving readers to a gentle reawakening.

Sangita Shroff
Dean & Director, Institute of Design
Nirma University, Ahmedabad

Editor's Note

Among the many tasks Sanjeev left unfinished before he tragically succumbed to Covid-19 was the publication of his PhD dissertation. I had discussed the task with him on several occasions, so I knew somewhat in detail what he had in mind. For the book, which is intended for a different target audience, he wanted to use the version of his first draft that he had prepared for submission to CEPT, Ahmedabad under the guidance of Prof. M.P. Ranjan. This version was written as a book and did not follow the usual format of a dissertation. Since both Prof. Ranjan and Sanjeev wanted to share their knowledge without the trappings of an 'accepted format', they believed that the narration had to be interesting for the target audience. Sanjeev moved on to Bansthali Vidyapith later and completed his PhD with Dr Himadri Ghosh as his guide. In our discussions with Dr Ghosh, he also suggested that this version would have better appeal as a book.

Since this task is seeing light posthumously, the few changes that I have made are essentially editorial. I have retained his tone of voice. He was a quintessential academic, a teacher par excellence, who wanted to share with the student community not only his thoughts but also the processes he had undertaken and his journey into the world of ideas which he has explained so simply but effectively in this book. The few additions that have been made to the original version are weaving in some parts of his Banasthali dissertation that would enhance the narration.

Sanjeev, I truly hope, I have not in any manner adversely impacted your communication with the readers. And you would approve the few editorial changes I have made. It would have been such a different experience if we had been able to work on this book together. But destiny willed it otherwise.

Nita Mukherjee
Jaipur

Acknowledgements

It is with mixed emotions that I present the book, *Design Education in India: Values of Socially Responsible Design.* This work is a revised dissertation of my late husband, who was a brilliant scholar, a passionate teacher and a lifelong student. I am honoured and humbled to have had the opportunity to bring his ideas and research to a wider audience.

From an early age, Sanjeev was deeply connected with the environment, and in later years, he developed profound concerns about its sustainability. The present work culminates his concerns and his experiences as a graphic designer. This book is presented with the hope that Sanjeev's passion for design and unwavering commitment to social responsibility continue to inspire the design community across the globe.

Sanjeev dedicated countless hours to researching, writing and refining his dissertation, which served as the foundation for this book. In his dissertation, he acknowledges that "I am grateful to all the experts who gave their valuable time for the interviews and, later, for respondent validation of the interview transcriptions. I would like to express my deepest gratitude to faculty, colleagues, and students at several design schools in India for showing interest, sharing documents and insights to provide valuable support during the fieldwork."

I would like to express my heartfelt gratitude to all those who supported me in this endeavour, with special appreciation to Sanjeev's parents. This journey would not have been possible without the unconditional support of Dr. Nita Mukherjee, author, researcher and social historian, as well as the guidance of Dr. Whitney Bauman, professor of Religious Studies at Florida International University, Miami. I acknowledge my gratitude to Sanjeev's colleague, Prof. Sangita Shroff, Dean & Director, Institute of Design Nirma University, Ahmedabad (India), who graciously wrote the Foreword of this book. I am also grateful for the blessings and encouragement of numerous people who are a part of Sanjeev's friends and family circle.

Finally, I am grateful to Routledge, UK, who saw value in this work and helped us bring it to fruition.

Shivani Bothra, PhD
Assistant Professor, Department of Religious Studies
California State University, Long Beach (USA)

Acknowledgments

Introduction

This book is an update of research undertaken for a doctoral degree at an Indian university. The author addressed it especially to the design academic community and design students. Having observed the devastation wreaked by consumerism resulting in irreversible damage to the ecosystems of the earth, the author firmly believed that unless designers are more socially aware and design products and services which minimise damage to the environment, conserve resources and preserve humaneness in labour relations, that issues of climate change cannot be addressed. The research was based in India and presents the Indian context, and the primary field study and research are India-centric. Still, parallels can be drawn with similar contexts and multiple locations. Hence, it is equally relevant for all contemporary design studies and training programmes.

This book begins with a brief history of contemporary design education in India to determine whether or not institutions that teach design impart values of socially responsible design to their students, the future design professionals. A review of the literature identified a paucity of empirical studies on various aspects of the content of design education programmes in India, especially about imparting values of socially responsible design. The study filled this important gap by analysing the mandates or vision/mission documents, curricula and pedagogies about socially responsible design values. Using a survey questionnaire, formal interviews and in-depth content analysis, the study sought to understand the challenges of preparing students to deal with the real needs of society and the environment, even as mass consumption remains the norm. Today, these issues have assumed great significance as the professional design has wide and complex interconnections with society and the environment at large, beyond merely those of production and consumption.

The book also presents three case studies of actual design education programmes where the author was the core faculty. The findings from the case studies demonstrated (corroborated by the experts) that values such as empathy, ethics and accountability are fundamental to socially responsible design action. Thus, responsible design education programmes ought to recognise and uphold such values at their core.

DOI: 10.4324/9781003383352-1

Among others, there are three key outcomes of this book. (1) The content analysed established that the intent of imparting socially responsible design values translates into the curricula and pedagogies only to some extent. (2) The work further demonstrated an evident gap between the articulated intents, their manifestation in the curricula and the pedagogic actualisation of imparting these values. (3) The research established the preeminent role of individuals—design educators and students—in instilling socially responsible design values.

Based on these experiences and years of his teaching experiences, the author suggests a future model. Future action in the context of design education needs to be both at the institutional and individual levels, where 'individual' refers to individual students and faculty members. To ensure consistent and responsible design input and faithful implementation of responsible design values, the book recommends a 'filter system' for the design process of socially responsible design. Broadly, the proposed filters provide ways of identifying design propositions, ideas and decisions that could contribute to irresponsibility and segregating them from those that ensure responsible design decisions.

A responsible design education programme has to incorporate certain filters in its *modus operandi*. The courses, individual assignments and especially independent projects that students take up in their senior years to apply and demonstrate their learning would need to pass through appropriate filter systems. This would also help ensure that courses incorporating responsible design values are not one-off, isolated or elective courses. To establish a design education system that is amenable to social responsibility issues, from the beginning till the end, one needs to incorporate the filter system into the assessment rubrics meticulously.

Filters could also be customised to vary their strengths for specific instances or projects. For example, a set of filters could be deemed suitable for first-year design students. As the students advance their learning and understanding, they may be given another version of these filters with more rigorous parameters.

These filter systems can equally well be applied to professional design practice. The versatility of such filter systems provides ample scope for development and pursuit of excellence. Independently or as part of collectives/networks, for example, design schools and professional bodies can support individuals to figure out ways of identifying, examining and integrating new approaches with the view to filter out irresponsible design from education programmes and praxis.

1 Prologue

When I arrived at the gates of a design school for the first time over three decades ago, I really did not know the profession I was taking up, except that I would get to 'create' something. And, of course, the campus and people 'looked different'; this gave me the intuitive feeling that it was probably because they 'think different.' It was an exciting proposition for someone just out of high school interested in doodling, drawing, colouring (painting), art and craft, and making things by hand. These almost seemed the prerequisites to succeed in the entrance exam to the premier design school of India—the National Institute of Design (NID), Ahmedabad—where only a handful of students were admitted each year. Incidentally, in 1987 (the year of my joining), NID completed celebrating its 25th anniversary.[1] The idea of an education in design as a profession is nascent, in comparison to the rich heritage of traditional crafts in India—the land of one of the oldest civilisations of the world. Design is a 'minority profession'[2] compared with other mainstream professions.

The two already-established areas can be broadly classified as education in the sciences and education in the arts, or humanities. These 'two cultures' (that extend beyond the Indian context) have long been recognised as dominating our social, cultural and educational systems. The 'third culture' is not so easily recognised, simply because it has been neglected, and has not been adequately named or articulated. In their report (Royal College of Art, 1979), Bruce Archer and his colleagues were prepared to call it 'Design with a capital D.'

The description of the 'third culture' helps to place design education in a broad educational framework with reference to science and humanities which seems to hold largely valid in India as well as other parts of the world.

When I went home for holidays during the first semester break at the design school, my family members, former high school friends and their parents were keen to know what I was going to do after becoming a designer. They asked: "Once you finish your studies, will you be making drawings and paintings; doing fashion design and tailoring clothes; doing interior decoration and making furniture?" These were mostly queries from well-wishers who were curious and concerned about my future. Their reactions indicated

DOI: 10.4324/9781003383352-2

the common impression of design as surface-level decorative styling to make things look good. Such queries and impressions about design and design education are prevalent even today.

Only halfway through the first year of the Foundation Programme, I was trying to understand for myself what design is or what it meant to be a designer. Without doubt, it is fundamental, yet a challenging question that probably all students go through in the process of 'becoming a designer'—what is design?

A broad understanding of what design is could help in expanding the scope and relevance of design and design practice, along with its social, cultural, environmental, ethical implications and responsibility.

John Heskett notes in his introduction to design, "Design is to design a design to produce a design."[3] Design can be referred to as a noun, a verb or even an adjective. In English, the meaning varies with context. For example, the designer is asked for a new cup design. The designer works to design new cups. Finally, one of the cups can become a popular design.

The following Figure 1.1 presents the search result for 'design' from an online visual thesaurus, which displays a web of terms, each of which can be explored to further understand the dictionary meaning of the word 'design.' This figure is a basic presentation of the meaning of design and its varying scope, relative to the web of contexts (Figure 1.1).

Designers, design educators and scholars of design have offered wider and skilful definitions of design which go beyond the narrow dictionary meanings.

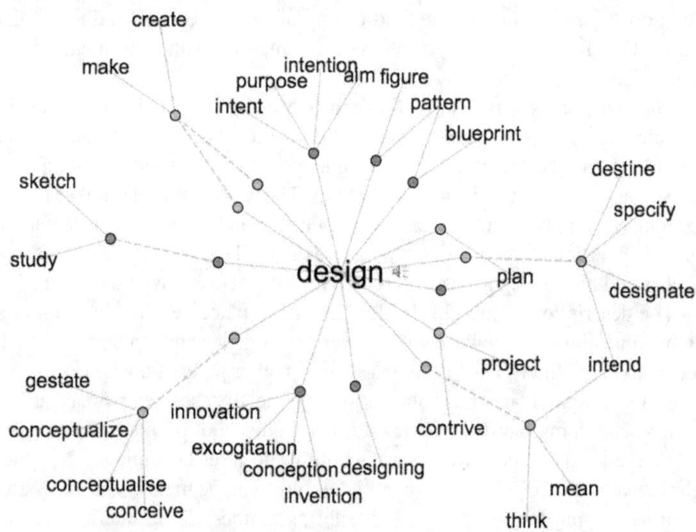

Figure 1.1 'Design' result for the word at *www.visualthesaurus.com* (Visual Thesaurus).

A few definitions of design introduced below to set the tone for subsequent discussions.

- "Design is … a natural human ability that almost everyone is designing most of the time—whether they are conscious of it, or not."[4]
- "To come up with an idea, and to give form, structure and function to that idea, is at the core of design as a human activity."[5]
- "Design, stripped to its essence," says John Heskett, "can be defined as the human capacity to shape and make our environment in ways without precedent in nature. To serve our needs and give meaning to our lives."[6]
- Philip Rawson states "Design is the means by which we order our surroundings, re-shaping natural materials to suit our needs and purposes. It arises at the interface between humankind and raw environment and expresses human intentions, desires, and hope."[7]
- In expressing "Design with a capital D," Bruce Archer and his colleagues articulated it as "the collected experience of the material culture, and the collected body of experience, skill and understanding embodied in the arts of planning, inventing, making and doing."[8]

The following conclusions can be drawn on the nature of 'Design with a capital D':

The central concern of Design is 'the conception and realisation of new things.' It encompasses the appreciation of 'material culture' and the application of 'the arts of planning, inventing, making and doing.'

At its core is the 'language' of 'modelling'; it is possible to develop students' aptitudes in this 'language,' equivalent to aptitudes in the 'language' of the sciences (numeracy) and the 'language' of humanities (literacy).

> Design has its own distinct 'things to know, ways of knowing them, and ways of finding out about them.'[9]

The design educator, MP Ranjan, describes "Design is a product of thought and deliberate action[10] that is composed by intentions and imagination and its effects are refined by explorations and sensitive judgments."[11]

Graphic designer, Milton Glaser shares his three favourite definitions,

> One definition is that design is the intervention in the flow of events to produce a desired effect. Another is that design is the introduction of intention in human affairs. A third rather elegant description is that design moves things from an existing condition to a preferred one.[12] This last one reduces the complexity of the idea, but I like all three definitions.

He goes on to say, "Design doesn't have to have a visual component. Ultimately, anything purposeful can be called an act of design."[13]

There are many variations besides the above-mentioned definitions. However, it is difficult to settle for a single definition of design even from the aforementioned. It seems easier to explain than to define, due to its contextual frame of reference within a wide spectrum. Over the years at the design school, in varying contexts, I came across many other 'definitions' of design: Design is cool; Design is culture; Design is cultural transformation; Design is change; Design is meaning making; Design is problem solving; Design is not problem solving; Design is the problem; Design is a way of life; Design is everything; and so on.

Figure 1.2 exemplifies a classroom brainstorming session on design and keywords associated with 'what is design?'

However, for someone who was studying at NID, the discussion about design would be incomplete without bringing in the metaphoric example of the '*lota*' at length. *Lota* is a rounded water pot typically made of metals like brass. This simple vessel can also be made of copper, stainless steel, clay, and even plastic. It can come with extended functionalities in various sizes, usually for containing and pouring liquids. A *lota* can be used for holding substances other than liquids also. Charles and Ray Eames referred to this in the India Report of 1958.[15]

> Of all the objects we have seen and admired during our visit to India, the *lota*, that simple vessel of everyday use, stands out as perhaps the greatest, the most beautiful. The village women have a process, which, using tamarind and ash, each day turns this brass into gold.

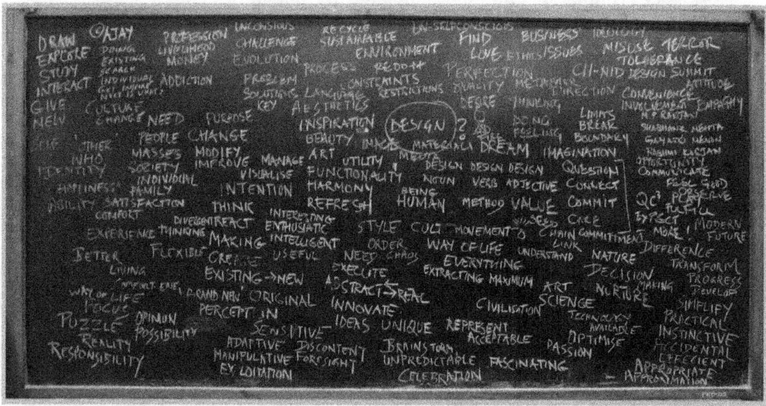

Figure 1.2 Black board generated through class brainstorming on the keywords associated with "What is Design?"[14]

But how would one go about designing a *lota*? First, one would have to shut out all preconceived ideas on the subject and then begin to consider factor after factor:

- The optimum amount of liquid to be fetched, carried, poured and stored in a prescribed set of circumstances.
  - The size and strength and gender of the hands (if hands) that would manipulate it.
  - The way it is to be transported—head, hip, hand, basket or cart.
  - The balance, the centre of gravity, when empty, when full, its balance when rotated for pouring.
  - The fluid dynamics of the problem not only when pouring but when filling and cleaning, and under the complicated motions of head carrying—slow and fast.
  - Its sculpture as it fits the palm of the hand, the curve of the hip.
  - Its sculpture as compliment to the rhythmic motion of walking or a static post at the well.
  - The relation of opening to volume in terms of storage uses—and objects other than liquid.
  - The size of the opening and inner contour in terms of cleaning.
  - The texture inside and out in terms of cleaning and feeling.
  - Heat transfer—can it be grasped if the liquid is hot?
  - How pleasant does it feel, eyes closed, eyes open?
  - How pleasant does it sound, when it strikes another vessel, is set down on ground or stone, empty or full—or being poured into?
- What is the possible material?
  - What is its cost in terms of working?
  - What is its cost in terms of ultimate service?
  - What kind of an investment does the material provide as product, as salvage?
  - How will the material affect the contents, etc.?
  - How will it look as the sun reflects off its surface?
  - How does it feel to possess it, to sell it, to give it?

Of course, no one man could have possibly designed the *lota*. The number of combinations of factors to be considered gets astronomical – no single man designed the *lota,* but many men over many generations. Many individuals represented in their own way through something they may have added or may have removed or through some quality of which they were particularly aware.[16]

The *lota* was a profoundly insightful example adopted by Eames to bring forth the complexities even through a simple, mundane, yet significant object of everyday use. Through this, Eames successfully draws the attention of the reader to the aspects of form and function; materials and finishes; tactile and visual appeal; issues of physics and chemistry of an object; aspects of gender, anthropometry, and ergonomics; physical and emotional relationships to an object; economics of producing, transporting, selling and buying; use and maintenance; even repurposing, salvaging and recycling; history and culture too. These could be part of the considerations of designing anything else in another context and are not limited to this specific object or country. At the beginning of the above quote, regarding 'designing a *Lota,*' Eames and Eames suggest that 'one would have to shut out all preconceived ideas on the subject.' However, they highlight the 'astronomical' 'factors to be considered' essential for any design work. They also acknowledge the important role of 'individuals' and the individual's 'own way' and particular awareness, in the process of design and the course of design development and modification. How far is it possible for an individual to 'shut out all preconceived ideas' while minutely considering 'factor by factor,' however objective one might try to be? The exhaustive list of issues that are listed for consideration, even for a seemingly simple object like the *lota,* is a reminder of the complexity of considerations which can very well have influences from past experiences.

Here I would like to recall the Symbol Design course during my third year at the design school. After having received the basic inputs regarding symbol design, the whole class was given a single design brief from one client. Each one of us came up with a distinctly different response and unique symbols. Surely some of the previous experiences, exposures, impressions, likes and dislikes—baggage from the past—influenced the interpretation of the brief (the design problem); hence, the distinctly different outcome (the design solution). Interest in what makes 'the difference' has been a continuous question of inquiry for me.

Close observations as a design student, and later as a visiting faculty to various design schools, as well as supporting references from several other sources, are woven into the texture of this book. They point to a strong curricular emphasis focused on the transfer of skills and techniques; know-how of tools and technology; and client presentation techniques, to sell ideas. Discussions related to ethics, values, beliefs of designers are avoided or limited to individual interests of concerned faculty members or students, without a definite academic guideline in these crucial, but seemingly personal, areas. There were specific courses that had more scope and opportunities to contemplate, question and discuss these values. Such courses were few and depended on the personality and initiative of specific course guides and mentors.

What guides intent, thought, action, judgement or sensitivity in an individual's action? Does not a personal belief system of ethical values have direct influence on an individual's outlook and design action? What influences the personal belief system of an individual? Should these not be areas of concern and discussion for integrating them into the education programme itself? These are some of the questions the book addresses.

Next, I would like to mention another observation from the *India Report.* The foreword to the report is a quote from the *Bhagavad Gita.* However, besides one quote, there is no other reference to anything of any religion. In the context of a country like India, where religious traditions and beliefs accentuate the socio-cultural backdrop, the *India Report* probably needed to accept this practical reality and outline a viable integration of religion and secularity into the education programme. It is worth noting that there is not even a mention of the word ethics in the *Report.* As invited experts from another country, Eames and Eames may have purposely avoided explicit references to ethics or religion in the *India Report* even though these are unavoidable complexities of designing for the real world. After writing the *India Report,* the authors may have realised the heavy Western influence on the report, due to their backgrounds. Therefore, they may have added the quote from the *Bhagavad Gita* as an attempt to fill the gap. It may also have been due to their own Western background where religion and ethics are seen as personal matters of individuals and not appropriate for discussion in a design school programme. Personal beliefs and ethical understanding influence one's point of view, understanding, action and reaction. Refraining from discussions about ethics or beliefs in the context of design and designer, as a part of design education, may be convenient but may not fully prepare the designer for the expected role and responsibilities.

As I was getting ready to start as a professional designer in the real world outside the ivory tower of the elitist design school, I was, like many other colleagues, left with an impression that we had been transformed into some kind of special beings with the ability to understand almost every problem around and hand down solutions for them all.

Definitely, this was not the case. We had a wide variety of exposure to understanding aesthetics but seemed to lack the understanding of ethics in the context of professional design practice. Therefore, we all started to fall back on our previous experiences and encounters with ethical issues and dilemmas in the context of the newfound role of problem-solving and creating through design. I felt that we were expected to either already have this understanding or discover it for ourselves to deal with the unavoidable personal, social, cultural, economic, political and environmental realities. After all, designers must deal with real people, their collectives and the surroundings.

To practically understand real-world issues and how they relate to professional behaviour, I thought of re-examining and, if required, unlearning some parts of what I learnt at the design school. I spent almost a year in villages in the arid zone of Rajasthan in western India. Thus, I had a chance to comprehend the ground realities about hunger, poverty, disease, death, and even caste and class divides between the poor and the poorest of the poor, child marriage, rape, ineffective governance, dirty politics, corruption, violence, and the value of half a glass of drinking water. I witnessed the lack of infrastructure, roads, electricity, water, hospitals, and political will… and the picture was very gloomy and depressing. However, the instinct for survival, hope and trust for a better future and other factors not known to me or beyond my comprehension made them continue. During my journey through the desert of sand and dunes of life, I met some common people with uncommon wisdom, commitment, perseverance, compassion, zest and unconditional friendship, which left a deep impression on my heart and mind. These experiences made me very restless to reflect and examine my responsibilities towards people and my role as a designer in dealing with problems of the world around me.

Sharing the desert experiences gives the opportunity to list some of the social and cultural issues highly relevant to a designer's responsibilities. The seeds for undertaking such an extended immersive experience were sown in the Environmental Perception course, the second to last course of the Foundation Programme at NID, towards the end of the first year of the undergraduate programme. This course was a three-week field experience in a rural microenvironment. "To perceive the environment, its various components and aspects, was the main aim of this course—Environmental Perception. Perception through observation, participation and drawing."[17] It was an intensive round-the-clock experiential learning, where the whole village was the classroom. Besides the two mentors from NID, local community members actively contributed to the learning process. "Allowing participation in the village activities was a fabulous aspect of the course—learning by doing—and doing for better perception—better perception to understanding clearly."[18] Through the planned assignments and evening discussions, the course proffered a design-biased exposure to social, cultural, religious, economic and environmental aspects in a simpler—rural—microenvironment. The group discussions and experience sharing revealed insights at various levels, against the individual's background and past experiences.

In retrospect, it seems that another planned exposure—Environmental Perception Part 2—towards the end of the design education programme may be significantly helpful in understanding the larger interconnections of issues for a better sense of their roles and responsibilities as professional designers. Even if the young designers were not directly working on particular topics, they would be at least mindful and considerate if they perceived how their design decisions would affect seemingly unconnected matters and, thus, take responsibility for their design actions.

Through the account of my journey into the inner world of design, the following are the four foundational assumptions of this book:

1 There is a 'baggage' of an individual's past experiences, beliefs and values, which manifests in a designer's feeling, thinking and working.
2 As an agent of change, the designer needs to consider a wide variety of personal, social, cultural, economic, political and environmental realities.
3 There is a compelling need for students to re-examine their ethical values and spiritual understanding in an increasingly globalised secular world

to cultivate values of social responsibility in the context of future design practice.

4 Design schools have the role, responsibility and unexplored opportunities to better prepare designers as catalysts or agents of positive change for the real world.

At this juncture, it is necessary to point out the keystone of my continuing inquiry. It is the lecture by Lynn White, Jr (a professor of History at the University of California, LA) delivered at the Washington meeting of the AAAS on 26 December 1966. The text of this lecture appeared under the title "The Historical Roots of Our Ecological Crisis" in the March 1967 issue of *Science*.[19]

Here are some key passages highlighted for further discussion:

- "Neither atavism nor prettification will cope with the ecologic crisis of our time" (1204).
- "Both modern technology and modern science are *Occidental*" (1204). "Human ecology is deeply conditioned by beliefs about our nature and destiny—that is, by religion" (1205).
- "What we do about ecology depends on our ideas of the man-nature relationship. More science and more technology are not going to get us out of the present ecologic crisis until we find a new religion or rethink our old one" (1206).
- "We shall continue to have a worsening ecological crisis until we reject the … axiom that nature has no reason for existence save to serve man" (1207).
- "Since the roots of our trouble are so largely religious, the remedy must also be essentially religious" (1207).

Here I want to point out three broad inferences from White's arguments:

1 Arrogant anthropocentric activities are at the root of our ecological crisis, nourished by greed.
2 Spiritual and ethical interpretations, understandings and beliefs are deeply ingrained in individuals' and collectives' feelings, thoughts and actions. Twisted and manipulated interpretations can become popular beliefs and action-guiding forces.
3 Ways to deal with worsening social and ecological crises will probably come from the root of the problem, which must be examined in new ways to find new solutions.

My inquiry focuses on ethics in design, especially in the contemporary context. This is in no way to indicate that aesthetics are irrelevant. A large body of academic and professional work mainly focuses on aspects of design and aesthetics in traditional and contemporary contexts.

Ethics in design and the subjectivity of the designer have become an area of increasing interest, debate, discussion and research. Typical areas of concern have been developing a code of conduct for designers and clients, transparency in business dealings and contracts, copyrights and plagiarism, the use of specific standards and specifications, etc. Discussions regarding the social responsibility of designers, especially in the context of environmental concerns, are gaining momentum too. However, little work discusses a designer's personal beliefs, values, ethics, secularity, spirituality, and consequential effects. This book examines design education and the importance of social responsibility of a designer in the context of personal belief system of ethics.

Notes

1 Based on the recommendations made in the India Report, the Government of India with the assistance of the Ford Foundation and the Sarabhai family established the National Institute of Industrial Design, as it was originally called, as an autonomous all-India body, in September 1961 at Ahmedabad.
2 Norman Potter described the profession of designers as a 'minority profession' in his book *What Is a Designer: Things. Places. Messages* (2nd ed.). London: Hyphen Press, 1980. p.13.
3 Heskett, J. *Design: A Very Short Introduction*. Oxford: Oxford University Press, 2005. p.3.
4 Nelson, H. G., & Stolterman, E. *The Design Way: Intentional Change in an Unpredictable World.* Englewood Cliffs, NJ: Educational Technology Publications, 2003. p.1.
5 Ibid., p.1.
6 Heskett, J. Op cit. p.5.
7 Rawson, P. S. *Design*. Englewood Cliffs, NJ: Printice-Hall, 1988. p.10.
8 Archer, B. Design as a Discipline. *Design Studies*, 1.1 (1979): pp.17–20.
9 Cross, N. *Designerly Ways of Knowing*. London: Springer, 2006.
10 My PhD thesis explored what influences the intentions and sensitive judgement in the context of thought and action, especially with reference to a design professional.
11 Ranjan, M. P. Design Thinking Models_Primer 2013, 2013. Retrieved from http://academia.edu/3848991/Design_Thinking_Models_Primer 2013.
12 Refers to Herbert Simon's description of design.
13 Glaser, M. *Art Is Work: Graphic Design, Interior, Objects and Illustration.* New York: The Overlook Press, Peter Mayer Publishers, Inc., 2000. p.8.
14. Ranjan, M. P. "DCC 2010: Foundation Batch 2009-10." *Design Concepts & Concerns*, 30 December 2009.
15. The India Report also known as "the Eames Report" is an important document in the history of modern Indian design Written in 1958 by Charles and Ray Eames at the request of the Government of India, the report outlines a programme for professional design training in India. (Eames and Eames, The Eames Report April 1958, p.63 in *Design Issues*, 7.2 (1991): pp.63–75. Print. This report formed the basis for the formation of the National Institute of Design (NID) in Ahmedabad India in 1961.
16 Eames, C., & Eames, R. *The India Report April 1958*. Ahmedabad: Institute of Design, 1997. pp.4–5.
17 Bothra, S. "Environmental Perception-23 Feb-12 March, '88." April 1988.
18 Ibid.
19 Lynn, W., Jr. "The Historical Roots of Our Ecologic Crisis." *Science*, 155.3767 (1967): pp.1203–1207. New Series.

2 Beginning of the End

Spaceship Earth

As you are reading this, it means that you are onboard this 'Spaceship Earth,'[1] and it is not completely broken apart. There is probably still some hope, and you are welcome on board as an astronaut.

Many of us have been intrigued by the idea of how it would be to take a ride on a spaceship but fail to recognise that we are already onboard one such spaceship. The concept of 'Spaceship Earth' became popular in the 1960s after photographs, taken from outer space for the first time, showed the smallness and fragility of our little planet. It is like a tightly sealed fragile bubble, hurtling through space, allowing only light to enter and heat to escape. R. Buckminster Fuller brilliantly and comprehensively wrote an *Operating Manual for Spaceship Earth*, since this spaceship did not come with one. In the manual, he explains how each one of us is an astronaut on this spaceship. He has also given a detailed historical account of how some of our ancestors and co-astronauts assumed the role of small and big 'pirates,' changing the face of the earth and pushing the future of life on this spaceship into jeopardy and annihilation.

The idea of Spaceship Earth is more than a cognitive expression to realise that our planet possesses finite resources common to all—humans and other beings for coexistence. Fuller's propositions may have seemed far-fetched to many in 1968 (the year I was born), but are obviously not anymore. Many others—individuals, scientists, economists, politicians, and activists—have expressed similar ideas. Global climate change and global warming have become key terms of reference and concern in discussions on the future of life on this planet, especially that of humans. The global environmental change is no longer a mere concept or calculation on paper. It is a bitterly experienced reality and is happening all around us. The severity of this is more evident in some locations than in others.

Many initiatives related to the above concern are being undertaken. One such example is 'Climate Voices,' an ethics-in-action project that was initiated in 2005 by a number of students. This project raises clear alarm signals through 600 interviews, recorded in 17 countries spread across all the continents, of people experiencing changes in their everyday life due to global

DOI: 10.4324/9781003383352-3

warming, or whose life has been shattered due to climate change. It also includes interviews with members of the scientific and expert community. The Climate Voices Project was also presented at the United Nations Climate Conference in Copenhagen in December 2009.

In November 2012, the World Bank released a report, titled *Turn Down the Heat: Why a 4°C Warmer World Must Be Avoided*, put together with scientific peer-reviewed contributions of experts from across the globe. This report spelled out what the world would be like if it warmed by 4 degrees Celsius, which is what scientists are nearly unanimously predicting by the end of the century (at the time of this writing), without serious policy changes. The 4°C scenarios are devastating: the inundation of coastal cities; increasing risks for food production potentially leading to higher malnutrition rates; many dry regions becoming dryer, wet regions wetter; unprecedented heat waves in many regions, especially in the tropics; substantially exacerbated water scarcity in many regions; increased frequency of high-intensity tropical cyclones; and irreversible loss of biodiversity, including coral reef systems. Most importantly, a 4°C world is so different from the current one that it comes with high uncertainty and new risks that threaten our ability to anticipate and plan for future adaptation needs.

A wide array of such material, information, data, case studies, conference proceedings, points of view, theories, arguments and counterarguments, have been presented at various forums at the local as well as global levels. Though the reality of global climate change has been widely accepted, it is not without contention. These counterarguments have ranged from viewpoints that the climate is not changing, to the acceptance that the climate is changing, but it is a natural process and not at all anthropogenic or human-induced. Such contentions have largely come from people outside the scientific circle or those on its periphery. A study published in 2013, in Environmental Research Letters, titled *Quantifying the consensus on anthropogenic global warming in the scientific literature,* concludes:

> The public perception of a scientific consensus on AGW [Anthropogenic Global Warming] is a necessary element in public support for climate policy … However, there is a significant gap between public perception and reality … Contributing to this 'consensus gap' are campaigns designed to confuse the public about the level of agreement among climate scientists.
>
> The number of papers rejecting AGW is a minuscule proportion of the published research, with the percentage slightly decreasing over time. Among papers expressing a position on AGW, an overwhelming percentage (97.2% based on self-ratings, 97.1% based on abstract ratings) endorses the scientific consensus on AGW.[2]

This study was an analysis of the evolution of the scientific consensus on anthropogenic global warming, based on peer-reviewed scientific literature from 1991 to 2011. The consensus over scientific facts on AGW is a necessary part of reflection on climate change.

> The mistaken view that there is no consensus in the scientific community needs to die a death. This view is taken seriously in some quarters – even some quarters that matter, like the US Senate – and it shouldn't be. It gets in the way of our real focus, the ethical demands associated with climate change.[3]

Science can only put forward the facts about what is going on and attempt to model or outline the consequences of climate change. Our actions or inactions are not only guided by what influences our perceptions and understanding, but how we set our priorities based on what we think is right, what we value, what really matters to us and what should matter to us.

Stealing the Future

> The worldly actions that we have taken *en masse* to sustain ourselves in the short term have increasingly been at the expense of maintaining the long-term sustainment of ourselves and the world around us. The greater our numbers and our technological capacity to misappropriate planet Earth's resources become, the faster we defuture ourselves.[4]

As a presenter at TED 2009, Yann Arthus-Bertrand pointed out how we humans, in the past 50 years, have altered our environment and the face of the earth more than was brought about in the entire history of mankind. With aerial footage from 54 countries, Arthus-Bertrand's documentary film, *Home*, gives a vivid account of how the Earth's problems are all interlinked and how we are going at a much faster pace than the planet can sustain. He says that our efforts may be directed towards improving our lives but shows his concern over widening wealth gaps and environmental degradation.[5]

The World Economic Forum released a report titled *Global Risks 2013* developed from an annual survey of over 1,000 experts from industry, government, academia and civil society who were asked to review a landscape of 50 global risks. The respondents rated rising greenhouse gas emissions as one of the three most likely overall global risks. Severe income disparity and chronic fiscal imbalances are among the first two.

Social and environmental ethics are closely interlinked. Issues of social justice that arise around global environmental change are far more complex than generally conceded in political discourse.[6] Let us briefly examine this through the example of the Kyoto Protocol, along with its background.

The Inter-governmental Panel on Climate Change (IPCC) put forward its first report in 1990. Two years later, the world leaders met in Rio de Janeiro for the Earth Summit. During this summit, the United Nations Framework

Convention on Climate Change (UNFCCC) was tabled for signatures. It came into force in 1994, and the 195 countries that ratified it are the parties to the Convention.

The UNFCCC acknowledged the factuality of climate change and the significant human contribution to it. It also recognised the greater responsibilities of developed countries compared to those of developing countries, based on the share of historical and current global emissions of greenhouse gases. The convention puts forward its ultimate objective to achieve:

> The stabilization of greenhouse gas concentrations in the atmosphere at a level that would prevent dangerous anthropogenic interference with the climate system. Such a level should be achieved within a time-frame sufficient to allow ecosystems to adapt naturally to climate change, to ensure that food production is not threatened and to enable economic development to proceed in a sustainable manner.[7]

In December 1997, during the third Conference of Parties (COP3), the Kyoto Protocol was formally tabled. It is an important landmark in the international politics of climate. The Kyoto Protocol is an international agreement linked to the United Nations Framework Convention on Climate Change, which commits its parties by setting internationally binding emission reduction targets. Recognising that developed countries are principally responsible for the current high levels of GHG [Greenhouse Gasses], emissions in the atmosphere as a result of more than 150 years of industrial activity, the Protocol places a heavier burden on developed nations under the principle of "common but differentiated responsibilities."[8]

The signing and ratification process was initiated on 11 December 1997, and intended to be effective from 16 February 2005. However, the mechanism of the Treaty to come into force was such that it could only happen if ratified by at least 55 industrialised countries (including countries in the transitory phase) that, together, accounted for at least 55% of total greenhouse gas emissions for 1990. The USA and Australia worked hard to weaken the Treaty in their favour. The refusal of the USA and Australia to ratify the Treaty is well known. Hence, with their enormous emission share in the context of the 55% rider, the Kyoto Protocol had nearly collapsed. But, with Russia's ratification of the Protocol, there were enough countries on board, and the Kyoto Protocol finally came into force in 2005. The EU won the right to function as a single entity with an easily achievable combined 8% reduction target. Australia did sign the Treaty in 2007 after managing to negotiate concessions, resulting in an allowance for 8% increase in emissions rather than a reduction. The individual emission targets do not seem to be based on the principles of responsibility, entitlements, present capacities, sustainability, or concern for the value of life. Many serious independent agencies and experts have compared the negotiation process of these targets to horse-trading. They hold the opinion that the Kyoto Protocol's target of 5% GHG reduction from the 1990 level is ludicrously small and endorse cuts of 60%–80% on 1990 levels by 2050. In December 2011, Canada withdrew from the Protocol and was the first nation to do so. With no intentions of meeting its committed targets, Canada withdrew from the Protocol just before the end of the first commitment period, thus, conveniently avoiding payments of crippling fines for failing to meet its targets. The USA, the biggest greenhouse gas emitter, has shown no intention of ratifying the Kyoto Protocol as of yet. The first commitment period ended in 2012. The second commitment period with amended emission reductions began from 1 January 2013 to 31 December 2020, as agreed by the parties in the Doha Climate Change talks in December 2012.

The factuality of anthropogenic climate change and the significant contribution of developed nations to it, along with their intensive industrialisation activities, were well established as a background to the Kyoto Protocol. Even with several lacunas, the protocol can be seen as a tiny step forward towards future negotiations and hopeful action. It was able to achieve several things; most importantly, it was able to set differential emission targets specific to participating countries along with a timetable. It also allowed for flexibility mechanisms for the parties to meet their commitments through International Emission Trading, Clean Development Mechanisms and Joint Implementation. Expectations from developing nations for participation in future rounds of emission cuts were also outlined.

However, the Kyoto Protocol cannot be seen as adequate and comprehensive, with several debatable issues highlighted earlier. Did developed nations weaken the Kyoto Protocol through their vested interest? Are the proposed emission cuts adequate enough? Are developed nations reluctant to take responsibility of sharing the greater burden? Are they really serious about the long-term sustenance of life on the planet?

Is it not morally adequate for the Kyoto Protocol and future negotiations to place a greater demand for emission cuts on those who have historically polluted the most and continue to do so? What are the responsibilities of the present generation of industrialised and developed nations which enjoy the fruits of development based on the ethically inadequate actions of their ancestors? Should these richer nations shoulder greater responsibility, as they are better positioned to act?

Should developing nations take a softer stand and give up some of their equity rights? Is it acceptable for developing countries to rampantly flaunt their uncapped emission limits in the name of development? Does the protocol adequately represent the concerns on behalf of the poorer, weaker and disadvantaged nations, where the citizens face the greatest challenges in dealing with repercussions of climate change induced elsewhere by those who enjoy the fruits of development? Are there any considerations for the unrepresented other co-inhabitants of this planet besides the humans? Is it acceptable to steal the future generations of their share of resources and hand down to them a battered and plundered planet?

On analysing the preceding questions, it is difficult to avoid arriving at the conclusion that selfishness, greed and manipulation are at the core of arguments against appropriate action based on equity, ethics and responsibility.

At this point, it will be relevant to bring up the example of Bhutan, a tiny Himalayan nation, which replaced its Gross Domestic Product (GDP) as an index to measure prosperity and growth with the Gross National Happiness (GNH) index, an idea first mentioned by Bhutan's King Wangchuk in 1973. This became widely known through an interview with the King published in 1986 in the *Financial Times* (of UK), headlining "Bhutan King: Gross National Happiness More Important than Gross National Product."[9] Quoting from Jeff Johnson's *Gross National Happiness and Development*: "Bhutan is the first nation to officially say 'no' and the first to challenge the idea that money is absolutely good." Additionally, in 2012, the government of Bhutan attracted worldwide attention by declaring its intention to convert its agricultural practice to 100% organic, paving the path to be the first such nation in the world.

The proactive action of Bhutan and the spirit behind climate change negotiations help to uncover the intentions that guide different actions. It is important to notice the contrast of ideals in these examples. For one, the emphasis is on happiness beyond materialism; while, in the other context, material prosperity receives prime importance even if it is amassed through greedy unethical procedures.

In the given status of the environment and the political will around it, the overall situation seems to be forbidding and difficult with complex challenges. But as humans, how did we land ourselves in such a mess? The answer does not seem to be as straightforward as the question.

Ever since humans became a numerous species, they have profoundly altered ecological equations with their unnatural treatment of nature. We may not exactly know when, where, or with what consequences, human-induced changes historically came about. "By the end of the 15th century, the technological superiority of Europe was such that its small, mutually hostile nations could spill out over all the rest of the world, conquering, looting, and colonizing."[10] Subsequently, by the 19th century, Western Europe and North America wedded science with technology. This union led to a widespread understanding that scientific knowledge implied technological power over nature. "Its acceptance as a normal pattern of action may mark the greatest event in human history since the invention of agriculture, and perhaps in nonhuman terrestrial history as well."[11]

By the end of the 20th century, we saw a growing concern for serious ecological backlash. The forceful impact of the human race has changed the very essence of the environment. In light of the facts stated above, it will not be an exaggeration to say that, certainly no other creature on this planet than humans have managed to foul their nest in such a short span of time. However, it will be worth mentioning the industrial revolution here. Though it may not have been planned,

> it was not without a motive. At bottom, it was an economic revolution, driven by the desire for the acquisition of capital. Industrialists wanted to make products as efficiently as possible and to get the greatest volume of goods to the largest number of people.[12]

The Occidental spirit distinctly dominated the whole process of industrialisation and mass production with advancements in modern science and technology.

The quest for industrialisation and mass production has become a global phenomenon, and almost all nations are either in the race or aspire to be in it. Obviously, mass production had to be supported by mass consumption. More production, for more consumption and, to promote even more consumption for more profits, creates the vicious cycle of even more production. The desire for more and more transcends all logical and ecological boundaries of need. Can a consumerist world predominantly based on infinite greed be sustained indefinitely?

The Model of Greed

A well-known quote from Gandhi is relevant in this context, "Earth provides enough to satisfy every man's need, but not for every man's greed." As the focus shifts from need-based actions to greed-based activities, the equation changes drastically. The single most important motto of such equations invariably is 'profit at any cost.' Social and environmental ethics are compromised and may hold little or no value in such equations of greed. Therefore, it becomes necessary to introduce the component of governance to keep a check on such activities. However, if the equation of production and consumption were based on harmoniously balanced real needs, it might not have been necessary to introduce the component of governance of any kind. Of course, aims, intentions and effectiveness of such governance are other issues that will be discussed subsequently. Following is a simple model to further explain the preceding points.

In the above model, 'Production' is used as an inclusive term but not limited to representing the nexus of raw material sources, production infrastructure, manufacturing units, industries, factories, producers, storage, transportation networks, technical and creative teams, companies, corporations, product and service providers, marketing, merchandising, retailing, customer care, after-sales services, etc. Similarly, 'Consumption' is used as another inclusive term for buyers, hirers, users, seekers, consumers of the products and services provided in tangible and intangible forms. And here, 'Governance' includes

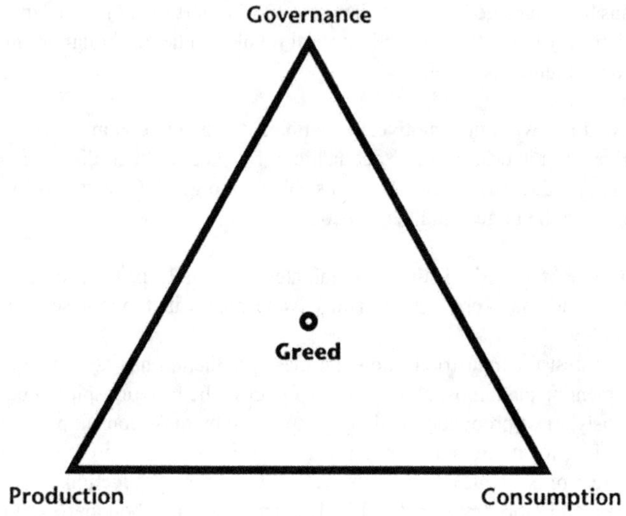

Figure 2.1 Model of Greed.

consumer laws, labour laws, antitrust laws, legislation, import and export regulations, memorandums of understanding, embargos, trademarks, copyrights, patents, licensing, taxation, at local, national and international levels.

The production nexus is supposed to serve the interests of consumers with due consideration for the environment and society at large. In the process of helping the consumer, this nexus serves its own interests of profit-making. In doing so, if it starts compromising its expected self-governed roles and responsibilities, external governance in its various forms needs to be in place at the helm of affairs as depicted in Figure 2.1, to maintain a stable foundation. However, if this triangle starts revolving around greed, the whole system can go for a treacherous spin.

The dimensions of greed can be many. Greed for possession, accumulation, consumption and control over physical, mental and conceptual forms can be unlimited within the extremes of human imagination. Consumers are a part of society at large; however, they are a class by themselves with access to resources which they exchange for products and services offered for consumption. With the power to buy, consumers greedily demand more and more new products, services and experiences at minimum cost. Such demands are essential for the sustenance and growth of the production nexus and feed their greed for more and more profits, their greed for a larger market share, their greed for access to cheap raw materials, labour and cost externalisation, their greed to control the greedy governance nexus, and so on. Though the governance mechanism is supposed to keep a close check on all-consuming greed, parts of this mechanism deceive the very purpose of its existence. The greed for undeserved power and unearned money, greed for favours from political and industrial lobbies, greed for illicit personal or professional gains, and greed to control others and their resources. Numerous similar greedy intentions deceitfully interfere with the expected role of governance.

The spirit of greed is all-pervasive in consumerist globalisation, and it attempts commoditisation by attaching the idea of value and profit to every opportunity and possibility. The process of commoditisation needs designs in the form of innovative ideas, creative thinking, production engineering and marketing strategies to translate these designs as tangible or intangible but desirable consumables. Nigel Whiteley, in his book *Design for Society*, differentiates 'consumer society' and 'consumerist society.'

> The consumer society is predicated on a market economy and so has been in existence for some centuries; consumerist society signifies an advanced state of consumer society and the market economy, in which private affluence on a mass scale is the dominant force in the marketplace.[13]

Since Whiteley's reflection at the end of the 20th century, the consumerist spirit continues to grow unrestrained across the globe, even in the present times. The faster pace and the wider spread of consumerist fervour and the 'designs' of the market on the consumers—plans to lure more and more people from every possible corner of this planet into the consumerist trap—with 'new' designs of products and services, we have arrived in what can be termed in its dual meaning as a 'consumerist world by design.'

Consumerist World by Design

Without the steady supply of design as the fuel, the fire of greed-based consumerism, the present economy would certainly collapse. "In an age of mass production when everything must be planned and designed, design has become the most powerful tool with which man shapes his tools and environments (and, by extension, society and himself)."[14] In the consumerist world we live in, design is marketed to define what is sexy and desirable, what is trendy and fashionable, brand values to aspire for and associate with. In fact, design touches almost every aspect of this consumerist world. Historically, we have come a long way, from the design of the essential tools by pre-historic people to futuristic design plans for a passenger shuttle to the moon. Indeed, the scope of design is vast.

The difficulty becomes acute if the word 'design' is used without reference to any specific context—used, for instance, as a blanket term to cover every situation in which an abstract of intent precedes the adaptation of something to an end—though designing is thus usefully distinguished from 'making' or from spontaneous activity. Beyond this point, the word must refer to recognisable products and opportunities or become hopelessly abstract.[15]

As one holds one's morning cup of tea or coffee and makes oneself comfortable on a piece of furniture to look at the newspaper or picks up the TV remote to know what is going on around the world—within these first ten minutes of the day, dozens of design services would have touched the person. The earthenware or ceramic design of the cup, the furniture design for the comfort of sitting, the interior and architectural design of the surrounding space, and the newspaper itself is a mix of graphic design, a complex hierarchical layout design of images and text, along with advertisement designs. There is the product design of the remote. Of the television set, the complex circuit design hidden behind its 35'screen and, the moment it is switched on, the flood of images, soundtracks, the news desk, programme sets and graphics, the makeup of the news readers, programme editing and video production, the commercials, the jingles, everything is the result of the innumerable design actions. And the day has just started!

As one gets ready for the day, goes through morning duties, puts on garments and accessories, cooks, eats and drinks, everyone is touched most intimately by a wide variety of product design, textiles and apparel design, packaging, information, advertising and graphic design and so on. The numerous smaller components constitute the considerable overall design experience. The texture of a switch, the curve of a handle, the smoothness of the rim of a drinking tumbler, the ease of the hook or the comfort of the lining of an undergarment, every detail is designed. It has profound effects on the conscious or subconscious minds of the consumers of these designs.

As the day progresses, one will utilise or be confronted by more and more designs. The complex automobile design and the shiny symbol design stuck on it, or, for that matter, even a locally designed bullock cart, public transport system design, graphically designed route maps, direction and signage system design, advertisement designs, visual merchandising and designs at sales points, planning and architecture design of the built surrounding, or the information architecture, applications and user interface designs of smartphones, and numerous other digital gadgets for personal use or in the public domain, everywhere there is design, design, design. We are in a consumerist world by design!

Design is omnipresent in this world. It may or may not manifest obviously, clearly or forcefully. Generally, it is taken for granted and goes unnoticed, unquestioned, unobserved or even unrecognised. However, designers—the people behind these designs, must be important, influential and smart. Now, one might reasonably ask, how do designers go about designing? And, even more ambitiously, enquire about what guides their acts of creation. What could be the roles and responsibilities of designers? These are essential questions that will be discussed in the following chapter.

Notes

1 Barbara Ward, an internationally influential economist and early advocate of sustainable development, used the term *Spaceship Earth* as the title of her book in 1966. Later in 1966, Kenneth Ewart Boulding, the cofounder of General Systems Theory, used the phrase *The Economics of the Coming Spaceship Earth* as the title

for his well-known essay. The idea of Spaceship Earth was largely popularised through the book by R. Buckminster Fuller titled, *Operating Manual for Spaceship Earth*, published in 1968.

2 Cook, J., et al., Quantifying the Consensus on Anthropogenic Global Warming in the Scientific Literature. *Environmental Research Letters*, 8.2 (2013): 024024. Institute of Physics. PDF file. p.6.

3 Garvey, J. *The Ethics of Climate Change: Right and Wrong in a Warming World.* First South Asian Edition. Continuum Special Priced Titles. London: Bloombury, 2008. p.13.

4 Fry, T. *Design Futuring: Sustainability, Ethics and New Practice* (English ed.). Oxford: Berg Publishers, 2009. p.110.

5 TED—Technology, Entertainment, Design—is a non-profit devoted to Ideas Worth Spreading. It started out (in 1984) as a conference bringing together people from three worlds. The TED 2009 conference was held Long Beach and Palm Springs, USA.

6 Hampson, F. O., & Reppy, J. *Earthly Goods: Environmental Change and Social Justice*. Ithaca, NY: Cornell University Press, 1996.

7 United Nations Framework Convention on Climate Change. Retrieved 3 May 2014 from http://unfccc.int/.

8 Kyoto Protocol. Retrieved 2 January 2012 from http://UNFCCC.int/kyoto_protocol/items/2830.php.

9 Weiner, E. *The Geography of Bliss One Grump's Search for Happiest Places in the World.* New York: Twelve, 2009.

10 White, L., Jr. The Historical Roots of our Ecologic Crisis. *Science*, 155.3767 (1967): pp.1203–1207.

11 Ibid., p.1203.

12 McDonough, W., & Braungart, M. *Cradle to Cradle: Remaking the Way We Make Things*, New York: North Point Press, 2013. p.21.

13 Whiteley, N. *Design for Society*. London: Reaktion Books, 1994. p.16.

14 Papanek, V. *Design for the Real World: Human Ecology and Social Change* (2nd rev). London: Thames & Hudson, 1985. p.ix.

15 Potter, A. Curriculum Assessment. In J. L. Green, G. Camilli, P. B. Elmore, & American Educational Research Association (Eds.) *Handbook of Complimentary Methods in Education Research* (pp.141–159). Washington, DC: Lawrence Erlbaum Associates: Published for the American Research Association, 2006.

3 Significance of Design

The omnipresence of design in this consumerist world is suggestive of the unquestionable existence of its creator-designers. Harold Nelson and Erik Stolterman, in their book *The Design Way*, describe design as 'an act of world creation' and a designer as a 'world creator' in the chapter titled "The Guarantor-of-Design"[1] (g.o.d). It is a widely supported point of view that the act of design is basic to all human activity and every human, in some way or the other, is a designer. Humans, in any time period, identify their needs—basic or beyond — and work towards planning, dreaming, creating, refining, discovering, recreating, innovating, and managing—and while fulfilling these needs physically or metaphysically, they assume the role of creator-designers.

As the human species multiplied in numbers and progressively became more powerful, the anthropocentric spirit gradually became the guiding force behind almost every human action. Thus, humans started designing and creating their own world according to their own image,[2] imagination and vision. It holds true, more than ever before, in the context of this consumerist world by design. But, as Potter said, even though every human being is a designer, "many also earn their living by design—in every field that warrants pause, and careful consideration, between the conceiving of an action and a fashioning of the means to carry it out, and an estimation of its effects."[3] Being a professional designer will be one such activity of earning a living by design. There could be many other professionals besides designers, like managers, teachers, authors, chefs, surgeons, and so on, who also embrace 'designer-ly' ways of knowing, thinking and doing to excel in their roles and perform the tasks at hand. Even though design is basic to all human activity, it is not necessarily, and directly, the profession of every human. Further, many professions may intrinsically use design or designerly ways[4], but, in today's world, the profession of design is distinct in itself. Nelson and Stolterman's idea of g.o.d. "is focused on the legitimacy and certainty of the designer's actions and accountability."[5] The present chapter discusses professional designers and their ways of conducting this act of designing.

DOI: 10.4324/9781003383352-4

Designer as Manipulator

Systems around us are constantly changing and evolving. These systems can be natural, such as the environment, or they can be related to humans, either as collectives or as individuals. This includes intangible mental systems, such as thoughts, desires, and feelings. Every entity is in a state of continuous transformation. Any act of designing essentially manipulates and attempts to direct this transformative process towards a preconceived and conceptualised desired realisation. The outcome and by-products of the manipulative processes may be tangible or intangible, ephemeral or perpetual, expected or unanticipated, good or bad, simple or complex. Whatever might be the consequences, the designer (as an individual) plays the key role of manipulator in such contexts. It is important to understand this dynamic nature of systems to effectively analyse and understand them.

Model of Manipulation

Imagine that you have been given the assignment of designing the Industrial Revolution—retrospectively with respect to its negative consequences; the assignment would have to read something like this:

Design a system of production that

- puts billions of pounds of toxic materials into the air, water, and soil every year;
- produces some materials so dangerous they will require constant and vigilant attention by future generations;
- results in gigantic amounts of waste;
- puts valuable materials in holes, all over the planet, where they can never be retrieved;
- requires thousands of complex regulations—not to keep people and natural system safe, but rather to keep them from being poisoned too quickly;
- measures productivity by how few people are working;
- creates prosperity by digging up or cutting down natural resources and then burying or burning them;
- erodes the diversity of species and cultural practices.[6]

To successfully complete such a design assignment certainly requires shallow vision and inconsiderate manipulation. Even without intending to do so, to take advantage of the immediate situation, what began as a part of the Industrial Revolution continues even today, only on a much larger scale in this consumerist world by design. Consumerism demands design and, in turn, design leads to further promotion of consumerism—a seemingly paradoxical situation but a reality.

> A created need is an imposed desire. It is a *faux desire*, which originates outside of the individual's own generative nature. It is preformed and impressed upon a person in their role as consumer or end user, through persuasion and manipulation.[7]

The model, illustrated in Figure 3.1, represents the manipulative interaction and the mutual influence of environment, society and individual on one another. A broad description of this model is followed by specific discussion on the role of designers as manipulators.

In the Figure, 'Environment' is used as an inclusive term to represent the environmental components of Spaceship Earth. This includes all the natural resources: the air we breathe, the water in its different forms, the lands above and below the sea levels, metals, minerals, oils in hidden depths, the aquatic and terrestrial plants and animals, the whole ecosystem and its delicate balance.

The term 'Society' in the model refers to the society of humans—the aggregate of human collectives of appearances, cultures, customs, practices, values, beliefs, status, class, natural or political boundaries and so on.

Humans are the only creatures on this planet with an extraordinary capacity to imagine, think, reason, argue, articulate and execute. Though the individual human being is a part of the global society, which, in turn, is a part of

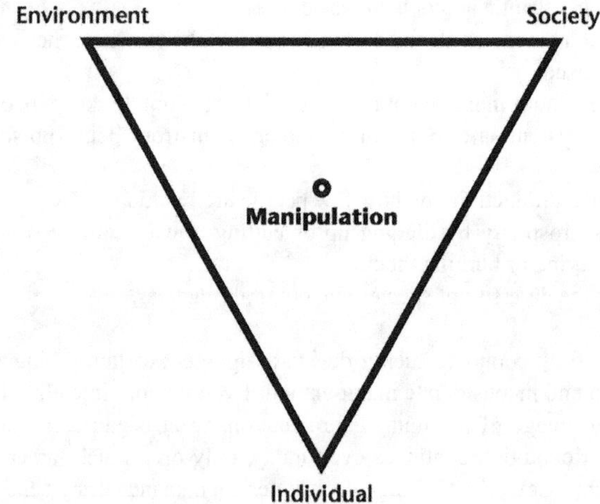

Figure 3.1 Model of manipulation.

the natural environment, the individual is also represented separately in the model at the pivotal position at the very base of this manipulative interaction. In the effort to fulfil the basic or advanced needs of individuals and societies, individuals either try to manipulate the environment, tame environmental forces or are forced to adapt themselves to the environment. The society and the individual are constantly influencing each other. The societal factors have complex and continuous influence on the thoughts and actions of its members, which, in turn, cumulate back as societal trends and processes. The same individual ends up assuming a wide variety of roles while navigating within and across different networks—consumption networks or production networks, sometimes in governance networks, or the networks of society and the environment at large. In the words of J. Krishnamurti, "It is always the individual, never the group or the collective, that brings about a radical change in the world."[8] Tagore placed a strong emphasis on the development of the individual creative spirit. The transformation and development of the individual were a central focus of educational experiments at Tagore's Shantiniketan and Krishnamurti's Rishi Valley schools. Gandhi's ideas of social change also centred on the idea of individual personal transformation. To further illustrate this point, here are Krishnamurti's words on the issue of individual transformation:

> So the first thing is to realize that the world's problem is the individual's problem; it is your problem and my problem, and the world's process is not separate from the individual process. They are a joint phenomenon, and therefore what you do, what you think, what you feel, is far more important than to introduce legislation or to belong to a particular party or group of people.[9]

Dimensions of personal belief system of an individual are discussed in a later chapter. An individual holds a pivotal position in the contemporary network as a whole.

Model of Contemporary Networks

Figure 3.2 illustrates the 'Model of Contemporary Networks' created through a combination of the 'Model of Greed' and the 'Model of Manipulation' described earlier.

To examine the interconnected complexities of contemporary networks, let us take the example of a phone—a device that was intended for voice conversation between two or more people, not in close enough proximity, to be heard directly. In 1876, Alexander Graham Bell was issued the patent covering the method of, and apparatus for, transmitting vocal or other sounds telegraphically ...[10] As we travelled across time, many others contributed to the design and development of the initial idea of Bell's phone. Earlier, children

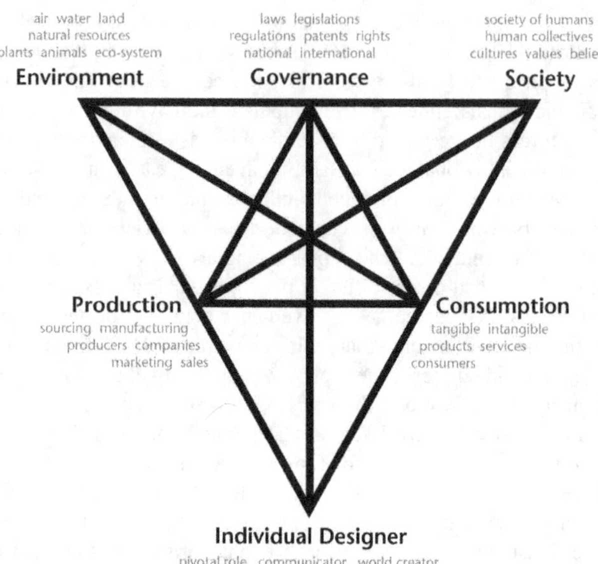

Figure 3.2 Model of contemporary networks.

were often seen making their own play phones by using a pair of paper cups and a long thread. They would attach one end of the thread to the base of one cup and the other end to the base of the second cup. At each end, the cup alternated between being a mouthpiece (microphone) and being an earpiece (earphone). To simulate the real phone, ringing and dialling were often vocally mimicked during play.

A phone still has a microphone to speak into, to transmit the voice/sound, and an earphone to receive the incoming audio. Along with it is a mechanism (like the ringer) to indicate an incoming call and an input mechanism (like the dialler) to put in the desired phone number for initiating an outgoing call. They function through wired and wireless networks. The basics of a phone remain unchanged, but the idea of the phone has completely transformed and changed.

There have been many techno-design avatars of the phone: rotary dialling, touch-tone dialling, re-dialling option, short-range cordless handset, IP phone, satellite phone and other such gadgets. The availability and affordability of a phone connection have also changed dramatically. The biggest departure was from the traditional wired landline phone to the wireless mobile phone. This moved the phone from being a fixed shared device to a personal portable device in the private domain.

The present consumerist market is flooded with mobile phones with varied combinations of features, in different form factors, and a range of accessories, to go with an individual's desired experience, affordability and the personality one aspires to project. This single product, which also happens to be a mobile phone, can also be a texting device, timepiece, alarm clock, torch, calendar, address book, compact camera, audio/video recorder, email client, web browser, personal digital assistant, GPS navigation device, portable media player and FM radio tuner, video and music player and gaming interface. This information, communication and entertainment device is still a phone. The phenomenal design changes mediated by technology,[11] in terms of form, function, features, service, use, message and meaning behind the phone have transformed the way individuals experience, interact, communicate and behave, and its social, cultural, economic, political, and environmental impacts.

Let us analyse some of these impacts, as the features on the mobile phone develop from being smart to smarter.[12] The context in which Bell's phone came to function, redefined it as what we now know as the mobile phone. Moreover, the new definition, which its developers did not completely envision, in turn, reshaped many aspects of daily life in ways that would not have occurred without the popularity and active redesigning of the mobile phone, its usability and manipulation of its social implications.[13]

One such example of socio-cultural impacts of the use of the mobile phone, frequently encountered on roads, campuses, working spaces, lobbies, cafeterias, trains, buses, and other public or private spaces is individuals' engagement with their phones. What is seen closely or from a distance are the movements of hands, changing facial expressions, conversations that look like eloquent monologues and virtual disconnection from the surrounding environment. This may presumably allow people to get more work done or utilise otherwise idle time. However, it inhibits interaction with people in close proximity, resulting in reduced interaction in public spaces. This, in turn, influences the behaviour of others around, since the person with the earphones plugged in or engrossed with device activity like talking, listening to music, watching a video, writing a text message or email, or simply exploring the device, seems occupied and therefore less approachable.[14]

Who is responsible for the changing quality of social interactions and its repercussions resulting due to new phones? Are the designers and makers of such multi-tasking mobile phones responsible for further isolating the individual from the surroundings? Does the individual user also share the responsibility of how and in what context it is used? Do such devices induce fidgetiness and preoccupation with virtuality? Are designers looking for new opportunities to create for the virtual world rather than the here and now world?

Furthermore, who is responsible for the health and safety of the active users and passive bystanders due to radiation from devices and mobile signal transmission towers? Who is responsible for the un-aesthetic alteration of our cityscape and landscape with these transmission towers? Who is responsible for complications due to repetitive strain injuries (RSI) like 'blackberry thumb'[15] or hearing impairment due to the use of earphones?[16] There are several other questions related to mental, physical or behavioural changes, but they are beyond the scope of this book.

Even toy phones have changed. The paper cup phones can rarely be seen. Now, children don't even seem to be interested in playing with toy cell phones. A two-year-old can be seen unlocking the screen of a real smartphone and navigating through the interface with ease, irrespective of the operating system of the phone. It is intriguing to see the agile adaptability of the product language, operative understanding and reinterpretations across cultures, gender, age, class and literacy barriers. Does this lead to homogenising experiences, eroding diversity or encouraging exchange and unity beyond boundaries and borders? Is it design universalisation? What kind of design language and whose aesthetic sensibilities and biases are being universally imposed?

For many, the mobile phone is a status symbol. Upgrading a phone is seen as a sign of personal prosperity and progress. The latest model of the phone loaded with features, irrespective of whether or not they are useful, is made into an object of desire. People seem to be watching whether you are carrying a smartphone or a dumb-phone.[17] Club or cult-like social subgroups emerge around users of specific brands, devices and services.[18] Companies plan and promote such branding, fan following or controlled user groups. Is it because the products and services are of exceptionally high quality or is it a designed manipulation of the vulnerabilities of user groups?

These companies also get involved in long-drawn rivalries, battle through advertisement campaigns targeting each other, and lengthy litigations for design, patent and copyright. Sometimes, even governments of different countries get involved in lobbying or legal battles. It will be useful to recall the model of greed discussed in the previous chapter. Is it worthwhile for the judiciaries to engage their valuable time in resolving the never-ending series of litigations and counter-litigations between two companies?[19] Do design patents delay and reduce access to designs, which would be otherwise beneficial to society at large?

Like other products, increasing demands for mobile phones have put immense pressure on resources and production processes. In a 2011 BBC news article, titled "Row over Exotic Minerals That Make Modern Life Tick," serious concerns over dwindling sources of rare earth elements and the technology metals raised by experts, industries and governments have been shared. With around a billion mobile phones being made every year, the 'volume of technology metals required is astonishing and the pace of demand is not letting up.' The article goes on to point out the need to make the embedded metals more accessible for recycling. Again, this calls for a technology-mediated design solution.

With planned obsolescence, consumers are easily trapped to discontinue a functioning mobile phone even in good condition. Further, with poor recycling facilities, useful materials are locked or lost forever in landfills or end up in incinerators. This may lead to serious contamination of soil, water and air. How can re-design contribute to solving various such environmental problems? Can designers counter the planned obsolescence with planned durability? Can design help in not just re-cycling but upcycling?[20]

Here the mobile phone is seen as a representative of how objects and their design profoundly transform individuals and societies. Furthermore, it gives a glimpse into the esoteric role of professional designers in the exoteric consumerist world. "The history of philosophy since Plato has tended to assign a secondary status to material and changeable things in favour of eternal and unchangeable ideas"[21] However,

> not only philosophy has failed to recognize the significance of things and their materiality—so has contemporary postmodern industrial design, whose products are devised principally to serve as signs rather than material things, as symbols or icons for their owners' lifestyles.[22]

Nevertheless, it may not be an exaggeration to consider the interconnected consumerist world to be a creation in the image, imagination and vision of the designer. With such powerful possibilities and immense opportunities to create, designers can be considered as creator demi-gods of the human-made world. It will be worth examining the dimensions of social responsibilities of designers as they create.

Elizabeth (Dori) Tunstall, a design anthropologist from Australia, in a public lecture titled "Cultures-Based Innovation: Theories and Practices"[23] in India in 2013, shared her experiences of working on the Aboriginal Smart Art Project in Australia. During her presentation, she referred to a designer's responsibility to seven generations. The immediate association was with seven future generations. But she gave a twist to this idea by dividing the seven generations into three generations of the past, three generations of the future, and the present generation. In the context of this book, her ideas can be expounded at two levels. As designers our responsibility is not limited only to the present but undoubtedly extends to future generations and the responsibility to carry forward the good design values and work of past generations. This same idea can be elucidated as the burden of actions of past generations that designers carry forward through the present generation to be a party in stealing from future generations.

It seems common for designers, even at the limited level of the particular project or programme, to be unwilling to accept full responsibility for the consequences of their designs. However, in the given circumstances of our planet, "these attempts by designers to divorce themselves of responsibility for the ultimate outcomes of their designs cannot be justified and are unacceptable, given the accumulating effect of small designs on the larger design of society."[24]

Redefining Social Responsibility of Designer as Creator

Victor Papanek, in his book *Design for the Real World,* has expressed his serious concern that recent design was neglecting the genuine human needs and satisfying only evanescent wants and desires. "The economic, psychological, spiritual, social, technological, and intellectual needs of a human being are usually more difficult and less profitable to satisfy than the carefully engineered and manipulated 'wants' inculcated by fad and fashion."[25] The first few sentences of the preface to the first edition of the same book by Papanek, say:

> There are professions more harmful than industrial design, but only a very few of them. And possibly only one profession is phonier. Advertising design, in persuading people to buy things they don't need, with money they don't have, in order to impress others who don't care, is possibly the phoniest field in existence today. Industrial design, by concocting the tawdry idiocies hawked by advertisers, come a close second. Never before in the history have grown men sat down and seriously designed electronic hairbrushes, rhinestone-covered shoe horns, and mink carpeting for bathrooms, and then draw up elaborate plans to make and sell these gadgets to millions of people.[26]

Such a trend is not limited to industrial design or advertising design alone. It extends into other arenas of design, including architecture. Issues raised by Papanek five decades ago seem to have escalated in both scale and scope.

> Designers, who themselves are controlled by those who want to fuel desire, discontent, greed and consumption, become willing participants in this destructive role of design. An enormously powerful tool for social development has been hijacked to become a servant of marketing.[27]

It is not that individuals and collectives have not questioned this or made efforts to change the course of action. However, all such efforts seem to have been dwarfed by powerful forces of greed and manipulation.

To dive into redefining social responsibility of the designer as creator, it will be worth identifying some of the key responsibilities of the designer towards other entities:

- Responsibility to the Client;
- Responsibility to the Consumer;
- Responsibility to Governance;
- Responsibility to Society;
- Responsibility to the Environment;
- Responsibility to the Self.

Responsibility to the Client: In almost every professional design assignment, there is a client, who entrusts the designer with the assignment along with a brief and agreements or understanding regarding other modalities. In most contemporary design practices, the designer displays prime responsibility to the client. For a designer, the client leads the nexus of production, described in the previous chapter. Since the client doles out the design fees, many designers can go to any extent to ensure profitability to the client. 'The client wanted me to do it' or 'the client's brief required me to do it like this' or even 'the client is God' is frequently echoed by those designers. Naturally, the designer has a responsibility to the client. What is the extent of such a responsibility? As Michael Bierut says, "The designer-client relationship can and should be a partnership. It's time to stop blaming the client when it's not."[28] However, he points out: "Our work can and should serve society. It should serve an audience beyond ourselves, beyond our clients, and beyond the next design annual." Bierut goes on to say that, "we designers, wanting to do what's right but afraid to make trouble, will keep sitting, maybe just a little more nervously, our fingers on our control panels, waiting for permission."[29] As a client exercises the options of choosing a designer, does the designer exercise conscious choice of working with the kind of client or assignment? What could be a designer's response to a client expecting 'green-washing' or adopting other unfair means or design of things that are dangerous to its consumers or society/environment in general? What really guides the ethical action of a designer?

Responsibility to the Consumer: The designer is responsible to the consumer for his or her design. Meeting the need, safety, aspired value, may be the basic expectation of a consumer. However, these may be superseded with the value of for profit-seeking clients. Is it the only goal to fulfil the desires of hedonist consumers or greedy clients? Is the designer responsible for promoting consumerism and the resulting social and environmental issues? Does the client, in its role as producer, marketer and promoter of the products and services, share these responsibilities? True altruism may not seem to be a viable business option today, but that still does not license reckless irresponsible greedy activities. Where does the responsibility of the designer begin and end? "The increasing reach and impact of design outside of its initial form brings with it an increased responsibility on behalf of design and the designer."[30] Designers must acknowledge their due and expanding responsibility. This begins with a designer's responsibility to gain trust through understanding and transparency. Transparency may not be the answer. However, it is the key for consumers to understand and trust the designs they buy. Thus, designers can responsibly explore 'trust as a function of design.'[31]

Responsibility to Governance: A designer is required to follow various local and global rules, regulations and laws, laid out by appropriate governing bodies to protect the consumer, society and environment. Is statutory compliance by the designer enough? What is the responsibility of a designer when hidden political agendas and commercial stakes rig the statute? Can the designer contribute to improving governance or fighting corruption? Maybe many designers need to overcome their moral reluctance for active political and social action through design activism. Fry, in his book *Design as Politics,* analyses the current 'solutions' to be 'utterly insufficient' in responsibly dealing with unsustainability. He emphasises the need for original and radical thinking, to tackle climate change-related larger issues and their politics. Fry positions design as a vital form of political action. He questions the very ability of democracy, in its present disposition, to deliver a sustainable future.[32] Probably there is a need for new forms of 'post-democratic politics' and responsible capitalism, where social justice and individual freedom are balanced, where sustainability is prioritised over maximisation of immediate profits.

Responsibility to Society: Design can affect society at large, even though every member may not be an active consumer. Numerous products and services, like the mobile phone, bring about multi-layered transformations (for good or bad), that, go beyond the location of its use, but spread out to unconnected remote parts of this globalised consumerist world. A product may be designed in the USA, assembled or produced in China and marketed in Australia or elsewhere in the world. Even the parts for assembling could be coming from multiple countries. Is the designer responsible for changes that happen in these far-off societies? Is the designer responsible for health hazards to the worker who is assembling the product as per design specifications? Is the designer responsible for unforeseen undesired effects or potential misuse of the design against society? Such questions are indicative of the "no finish line—no endgame"[33] of the expansive nature of responsibilities and goals. Expounding on the idea of abundance through upscaling, McDonough and Braungart emphasise the need to "honor and acknowledge everything the world can be and have within it if 'Cradle to Cradle' design were to truly take hold,"[34] and the aim of achieving "the goal of the upcycle [which] is a delightfully diverse, safe, healthy and just world with clean air, water, soil and power—economically, equitably, ecologically, and elegantly enjoyable."[35]

Responsibility to the Environment: A designer owes immense responsibility for not just social but environmental consequences of design specifications and actions. Many researchers of diverse disciplines have raised alarming sounds regarding other impacts of design. For example, Rogers states: "The new worldview teaches us that illness is not only attributed to toxins, germs, and bacteria but also to chronic dysfunctional emotional energy patterns and unhealthy ways of relating to ourselves and the environment."[36] The gravity of the environmental crisis and its consequences currently faced by the human and non-human world has been outlined in the previous chapter. If we can find ways to design better environments and systems of communications, we have the opportunity to improve the quality of people's lives and the life systems of the planet. Can the designer create with greater sensitivity and accountability? Can design heal the pre-existing environmental injuries and social sicknesses? To what extent is the designer, and the designer alone, responsible for the design consequences?

Responsibility to Self: The starting lines of William Blake's famous poem *Auguries of Innocence*, illustrates the paradoxical need for responsibility to oneself by seeing the larger interconnectedness to respond and be responsible to others.

> To see a world in a grain of sand
> And a heaven in a wild flower,
> Hold infinity in the palm of your hand,
> And eternity in an hour.

A designer's responsibility towards oneself can be the key to manifestation of holistic responsibility in its role of creator-designer. In *Citizen Designer: Perspectives on Design Responsibility,* Michael Schmidt through his contribution, titled "Responsibility Answers Absurdity" emphasises,

> what we do as designers is becoming more and more a global act: whether we're talking about Web or brand design for transnational corporations. Importantly, our productions are not limited to the bounds of any one given nation-state or cultural milieu.[37]

Schmidt calls for a serious self-reassessment by designers, of the underestimation of importance, of their own roles and says "we can tell ourselves that we're just one small piece of the puzzle; in which case we need a good look at the picture on the box."[38] A designer's personal beliefs, orientation and understanding of justice, equity, economics, class, caste, colour, gender, religion and politics, influences and reflects in the creation process. A designer, in the decision-making process, may often find oneself at the crossroads of conflicting situations.

When opposing interests, viewpoints, and ideologies come into contact, absurd things occur. One side of the dichotomy, for instance, may not even be aware of the other to any meaningful extent. Peacefully and equitably acquainting opposing forces is not something that the human race does well. We tend to get that one wrong, more times than not. Through responsible and reasoned attention to such absurdities, we might just be able to make some sense.

The critical question that emerges here is: What influences the orientation of the personal belief system of a designer? Most of the questions raised above relate to ethics and responsibility of designers, intertwined with other complexities of contemporary networks, without clear-cut answers. However, these questions call for discussions to understand what really influences the values of social responsibility for an individual designer. Values of social responsibility seem to be deeply rooted in the individual's personal belief systems.

Notes

1 Nelson, H. G., & Stolterman, E. Op cit. p.239.
2 Drawn upon the idea from Genesis 1:27 "God created man in his own image."
3 Potter, N. Op cit. p.13.
4 In the late-1970s, Prof. Bruce Archer initiated the inquiry of 'designerly ways of thinking and communicating' and it could be different from, but as powerful as, scientific and scholarly methods of inquiry when applied to its 'own kinds of problems.' Prof. Nigel Cross clearly articulated this concept in a paper titled "'Designerly Ways of Knowing" published in *Design Studies*, 3.4 (1982): pp.221–227. Subsequently, Professor Cross authored a book, *Designerly Ways of Knowing* published by Springer, 2006.
5 Nelson, H. G., & Stolterman, E. Op cit. p.242.
6 McDonough, W., & Braungart, M. *Cradle to Cradle: Remaking the Way We Make Things* (1st ed.). New York: North Point Press, 2002. p.18.
7 Nelson, H. G., & Stolterman, E. Op cit. p.139.
8 Krishnamurti, J. *Social Responsibility: A Selection of Passages for the Study of the Teaching of J. Krishnamurthy*. Eds. Douglas Evans and Forde Steen. Chennai: Krishnamurti Foundation India, 2007.
9 Ibid., p.30.
10 Bell, A. G. Improvement in Telegraphy, March 7, 1876.
11 Peter-Paul Verbeek's theory of 'Technological Mediation' describes the mediating role of technological devices in the human-world relationship and social transformation. Verbeek builds on the work of Don Ihde, Bruno Latour and Albert Borgmann.
12 Refers to transition of older 'feature phones' to newer 'smart phones' paving way for futuristic developments, for example Pranav Mistry's 'Sixth Sense' project at MIT Media lab.
13 Draws upon Verbeek's expansion of Ihde's reference to the initial intent of the telephone as a contrivance and its redefinition in his book *What Things Do: Philosophical Reflections on Technology, Agency, and Design.*
14 Ross, P. R. Ethics and Aesthetics in Intelligent Product and System Design (Diss). Eindhoven University of Technology, Eindhoven, December 17, 2008. p.35.
15 Injury caused by the frequent use of the thumb(s) to press buttons on PDAs, smartphones, or other mobile devices. The name of the condition comes from the BlackBerry, a popular brand of smartphones.
16 A class-action lawsuit seeking to hold Apple Inc. responsible for possible hearing loss caused by using its popular iPod music player in conjunction with earphones.
17 The older kinds of mobile phones with limited features and capabilities which are not enough to qualify as a smartphone.
18 Common examples would be users of operating systems like Android and iOS, loyal brand followers of Apple and its iconic iPhone, and strongly emerging brands like Samsung, against once very popular Blackberry with its BBM (BlackBerry Messenger service) and earlier market leaders like Nokia and Motorola.
19 Refers to lawsuits between Apple Inc., and Samsung Electronics Co. Ltd., regarding design of smartphones and tablets. Since 2011, the two companies have been engaged in legal battle in courts of United States, South Korea, Japan, Italy, Germany, France, the Netherlands, Britain and Australia.
20 Expanded as 'Virtuous Cycle' by McDonough and Braungart, *The Upcycle) Beyond Sustainability – Designing for Abundance,* a follow-up to their earlier (2002) claim

to fame book (*Cradle to Cradle*): *Remaking the Way We Make Things*, urging 'Reduce, Reuse, Recycle' and avoiding downcycling.

21 Verbeek, P. P. *What Things Do: Philosophical Reflections on Technology, Agency, and Design* (R. P. Crease, Trans.). Pennsylvania: Pennsylvania State University Press, 2005. p.1.

22 Ibid., p.2.

23 Lecture held at the Indian Institute of Crafts and Design in Jaipur on 14 February 2013.

24 Nelson, H. G., & Stolterman, E. Op cit. p.243.

25 Papanek, V. *Design for the Real World: Human Ecology and Social Change* (2nd revised). London: Thames and Hudson, 1985. p.15.

26 Ibid., p.ix.

27 Trivedi, K. Sarvodaya – Betterment of All *ICSID News*, February 2003.

28 Bierut, M. *Seventy-Nine Short Essays on Design* (1st ed.). New York: Princeton Architectural Press, 2007. Print.

29 Ibid., p.22.

30 Burnham, S. *Trust Design – Part 1*: "Trust, Design and Aging." The Netherlands: The Netherlands Institute for Design. 2011. pp.51–58.

31 Trust Design is also an initiative of Premsila, Dutch Platform for Design and Fashion, to re-examine design values in the context of trust and to explore trust as a function of design.

32 Fry, T. *Design as Politics*. Oxford and New York: Berg Publishers, 2010.

33 McDonough, W., & Braungart, M. *The Upcycle: Beyond Sustainablity - Designing for Abundance*. New York: North Point Press, 2013. p.12.

34 "Walter Stahel, Swiss architect, first used the term 'cradle back to cradle' in 1982 to describe what he saw as the only path to a sustainable economy, one in which durable goods are used in continuous loops as opposed to relying on end-of-pipe solutions. Around the same time, the chemist Michael Braungart promoted material recycling as a 'cradle back to cradle' loop, again as a reaction to the end-of-pipe issue of 'cradle to grave'" ("Cradle to Cradle"). The idea of 'doing less bad' was countered with 'doing more good.' Later in 2002, McDonough and Braungart developed Cradle to Cradle® as design framework and subsequently a C2C certification system.

35 McDonough, W., & Braungart, M. *The Upcycle: Beyond Sustainability – Designing for Abundance*. New York: North Point Press, 2013.

36 Rogers, C. A. Healing with Design. In S. Heller & V. Vienne (Eds.) *Citizen Designer: Perspectives on Design Responsibility* (pp.36–41). New York: Allworth Press, 2003.

37 Schmidt, M. Responsibility Answers Absurdity. In S. Heller & V. Vienne (Eds.) *Citizen Designer: Perspectives on Design Responsibility*. New York: Allworth Press, 2003. p.124ff.

38 Ibid., p.125.

4 Personal Belief System

Before going into examining some key components of personal belief systems, it is necessary to expand on what these imply. Bob Burg, author of *Adversaries into Allies*, describes 'belief' as: "the truth *as one understands the truth* to be." Though truth itself is a mere fact—neutral, without feeling, just as is, an individual with an "emotional mind … takes its beliefs to be absolutely true, and so discounts any evidence to the contrary."[1] Therefore, a person's belief is essentially the subjective expression of his or her 'own truth' derived from unique ways of seeing and making meaning of their experiences in order to organise their world. Carol S. Dweck, author of *Self-theories*, and researcher over several decades in the field, points out:

> [Jean] Piaget, the titan of cognitive developmental psychology, realized near the end of his life that simply focusing on logical thinking and its development was not enough. He came to believe that the meaning systems that people adopted were as important or even more important in shaping their thinking.[2]

Dweck spells out in her book how people's beliefs about themselves (their *self-theories*) can create different psychological worlds, leading them to think, feel and act differently in identical situations. Though each one of us creates our own unique personal belief system, we often tend to believe that everyone else sees the world in the same way as we do. And we overlook the fact that the other person too sees the world, in their own unique way, with the belief that their perspective is the right one.

Burg, another author who has worked extensively on the impact of personal belief systems on one's work, life and attitude, also points out: "Each one of us sees the world in a unique way based on a combination of upbringing, environment, schooling, popular media, and the people with whom we associate."[3] To explore the personal belief system specifically in the context of design education, let us discuss the broad categories of upbringing and the socio-cultural maze that covers religion, ethics, morality and spirituality.

DOI: 10.4324/9781003383352-5

Upbringing

It is a widely accepted fact that, for an individual, the initial years of growing up as a child have an everlasting impact and have complex implications, which will colour his or her thoughts and actions even as an adult.

> Our basic belief system is formed at a very young age. Many psychiatrists state that age as four years though I suspect the process begins even earlier! Our belief system is first given to us by our family and then finely chiselled by our environment, associations and life experiences.[4]

Human offspring require a prolonged 'upbringing' period which, in turn, extends the period and opportunities of impact during upbringing. Since humans, by nature, are social beings, the individuals—parents, guardians, extended family members, day care givers, baby-sitters, teachers—who directly take care or oversee the upbringing of a child, weave a vivid impression on the growing individual with their own individuality, social, cultural and other personal beliefs. The toys, games, stories, playmates, role-plays, observations of people, surrounding objects and environment, all contribute to impression formations. With reference to Piaget's 'Theory of Knowledge Types,' children start with acquiring physical knowledge, subsequently engage in logico-mathematical knowledge and are then ready to deal with the complexities of social knowledge—human emotions, social cues, cultural undercurrents. Assimilation of such knowledge, likc scaffoldings, builds over previous experiences and grows in complexities, but does not change in basic structure.

Socio-cultural Background

Society and culture are closely interrelated and highly interdependent. Here, the term 'socio-cultural' is used to broadly encompass a wide range of social and cultural milieu that a person manoeuvres through to deal with everyday life. As the child grows, many diverse socio-cultural encounters and experiences shape the future adult. There is a dynamic interactive relationship between an individual and her socio-cultural surrounding.

> When sociologists talk about culture … they usually mean the four things: norms, values, beliefs, or expressive symbols. Roughly, norms are the way people behave in a given society, values are what they hold dear, beliefs are how they think the universe operates, and expressive symbols are representations, often of social norms, values, and beliefs themselves.[5]

However, from the standpoint of humanities, culture manifests through music, performing arts, fine arts, architecture, design, literature and philosophy.

Culture is a broad-ranging term that can be explicit and expressive as well as implicit and indicative of human society and its meaning-making processes. A society can be defined as a collective of people who interact over a shared common culture. This could be based on: genealogy, religion, sexual orientation, affluence level, common interests, profession, geographical or political boundaries and other such distinct factors.

Society and culture can be seen as a highly intertwined complex maze, where the individual members of the collective searches for the meaning to action and anchors their beliefs. Different areas of the socio-cultural maze have varying levels of complexities and the encounters have different resulting impacts on the individual. This results in making unique contributions to the personal belief system.

Let us examine a few areas of this maze.

Stimulus: The social environment may be such that an individual is either positively stimulated or demotivated and challenged in a particular direction. For example, there is a high possibility of the development of creative abilities in an individual growing up in an environment stimulated by music, art and aesthetics.

Prejudices: Socio-cultural prejudices towards class, caste, colour, gender, physical appearance, social status, material possessions, etc., often influence the self-esteem of an individual. These can have far-reaching impacts on understanding social justice.

Resources: The abundance or scarcity of resources and their treatment, experienced by a growing individual, guides her outlook towards the material world (including money) and natural resources. The kind of resources and their availability can influence the access to opportunities as well.

Role Models: The younger members of a collective often look to grown-ups as role models. A member of the family, a teacher at school or a leader at a social, political or religious organisation, or even a designed fictitious character can leave far-reaching impressions on the minds of individuals with regard to appropriate behaviour, ethics, values, morality, justice and equity.

Religion: Religion (including atheism) is a dominant and highly complex area in this socio-cultural maze. It is apparently an arguable, yet an influential force in shaping individuals in what they are. Observations and experiences surrounding religion provide a certain kind of acquired set of beliefs, values, habits and feelings that get unconsciously imbibed during early childhood. Further, when young minds begin to develop, they are fed with sets of ideas that represent the dominating religion and value system. Still later, when young people start to think independently, they may not be aware of how much they are already submerged in the values of their culture, in general, and religion, in particular. However, as adults, they may accept or reject a specific idea or belief.

An individual is an integral part of society, and the science of sociology has incontrovertibly settled on the fact that society and religion share a reciprocal relationship. Therefore, in the ongoing discussion of the personal belief system, it is imperative to bring in the critical role of religion in developing the consciousness of individuals.

Religious beliefs and values serve as the bedrock for building any society and stabilising culture. To be more explicit, we should examine how different religious ideologies reflect in the formation of societies and cultures. On the one hand, there are traditions in which all creatures, including humans, have shared equal rights. These traditions emphasise renunciation and self-restraint. Such traditions manifest in societies less dependent on material goods—valuing the sacredness of the environment and maintaining a balance between need and greed. On the other hand, religious traditions which sanction the superiority of humankind over nature and possess an indifferent or uncaring attitude towards material and environment, evolve into a highly consumerist, materialist society. Understanding and belief in specific ideologies have guided human actions down the ages as much as they do today.

But how do religion and society act upon each other? Karl Marx (1818), the German revolutionary socialist, sheds light on the religion-society relationship: "Religion is merely an epiphenomenon that is a mere reflection of more fundamental social realities"[6] While Max Weber another German sociologist and political economist, counters Marx's significant idea and states, "Religious beliefs and practices play a critical role in change and evolution of societies." Regardless of whether we go with Marx or Weber, they both point towards the mutual and complementary relationship between society and religion. Moreover, since individuals are an indispensable part of both religion and society, one's personal belief system is not left untouched by the critical forces of religion and society.

Despite the significant role of religion in forming societies and cultures, many recent researchers have also illuminated the paradoxical, conflicting force of religion contributing to the disintegration of societies and cultures. Due to the increasing forces of secularisation in the modern industrial age, there is a waning power of religion in structuring societies, cultures and lives of people today. In *The Sacred Canopy*, an important work in the sociology of religion by the noted sociologist Peter Berger, the author defines secularisation as "the process by which sectors of society and culture are removed from the domination of religious institutions and symbols." Therefore, a broad understanding of spiritual and ethical values, without identifying oneself with any specific religion, is more accepted in an increasingly secular world today.

Ethics: Any discussion of secular ethics demands a philosophical exposition of three classical traditions with distinct characteristics—Deontologist, Consequentialist and the Utilitarian. Each of these three traditions proposes a theory of right or wrong conduct built on humanitarian grounds and free from any religious trappings. The first category discussed here is of Deontologist—it is a duty to always act according to what is morally right, irrespective of the consequences. Second is the Consequentialist—any action is right or wrong based on an evaluation of the consequences. Good consequences direct the action, whereas actions with undesirable results are considered morally wrong and, hence, to be avoided. The third category is the Utilitarian—emphasising the moral behaviour of individuals that leads to the greatest good for the greatest number of people.

Even from the brief annotation on ethical theory, one comes across the word 'moral' twice. What does this mean? There is certainly a connection between the two interrelated terms—ethics and morality—and it is worth exploring the connection. On the one hand, ethics is commonly considered as the foundation of morality and, on the other hand, moral action is also understood as the basis of ethics. In fact, both the terms are often used interchangeably; yet a subtle distinction can be drawn from these two notions. Ethics is an external code of conduct and is particularly related to standards set by society and culture. Morality, then, is internal and specifically associated with an individual's personal beliefs and values guided by the forces of ethics.

This conventional understanding of ethics and morality forms the basis of applied ethics, which could presumably be a guide in restructuring the design education programme and extend to professional design practice. Applied ethics is a relatively recent branch of philosophical tradition that deals with application of ethical theories (as briefly enunciated above) to moral dilemmas in specific contexts of professional and personal life. This implies the morally correct course of action and value judgement. A few examples are: business ethics which deals with moral and ethical problems of the business environment; professional ethics, which relates to issues of specific professions like medical ethics in the case of a medical practitioner, a code of conduct for architects and so on. Regardless of the field of work, what is most crucial is an individual's personal ethics or a worldview of shared ethics, which acts on various levels even beyond one's personal life.

Spirituality: The dual concepts of materiality and spirituality are embedded in humanistic beliefs and everyday living. The present work began with a lengthy discourse on the material world and its aftermath and continues the discussion to the other realm, i.e., spiritual. Andrew Wright, in his notable work *Spirituality and Education,* points out,

> at both popular and academic levels a reaction against the failures of modern rationalism, materialism and capitalism, coupled with a newfound freedom from the dogmas of traditional religious discourse has helped create a renewed interest in spiritual questions, issues and values.[7]

Therefore, spirituality leads to a 'reconnection' with one's own essence, to understand who one really is, where one comes from, what the meaning of life is, and what one's task or duty in life might be.

In the book *Ethics of the New Millennium,* the well-known spiritual leader, the Dalai Lama, notes that spirituality emphasises humanistic qualities such as love, compassion, patience, forgiveness, responsibility, harmony and concern for others. Although spirituality is inclusive, it encompasses a broad variety of aspects concerning human life. Research over several years points to the spiritual crisis in the present design education system and proposes a compelling need to integrate elements of spirituality for an integrated development—physical, mental, emotional, intellectual and spiritual health—of an individual.

The development of ethical and spiritual beliefs, as a part of the personal belief system of an individual, is further explored in this book and will be discussed in detail in the context of design education and praxis in subsequent chapters.

Notes

1 Goleman, D. *Emotional Intelligence: Why It Can Matter Than IQ*. London: Bloomsbury Publishing, 1996.
2 Dweck, C. S. *Self-Theories: Their Role in Motivation, Personality, and Development.* New York: Psychology Press, 2000.
3 Burg, B. *Adversaries into Allies: Win People over without Manipulation or Coercion.* New York: Portfolio Hardcover, 2013. p.14.
4 Burg, B. "Belief Systems." Retrieved 30 June 2010 from http://www.burg.com/2010/07/belief-systems.
5 Griswold, W. *Cultures and Societies in a Changing World* (4th ed.). Thousand Oaks, CA: SAGE Publications, 2012. p.3.
6 Livingston, J. C. *Anatomy of the Sacred: An Introduction to Religions* (6th ed.). Upper Saddle River, NJ: Pearson, 2008. p.126.
7 Wright, A. *Spirituality and Education.* e-library. London: Routledge, 2004. p.2.

5 Contemporary Design Education and Concern for Social Responsibility

Introduction

This chapter focuses on the roots of modern design education in India and its developments in the contemporary context. I examine how social responsibility is perceived in contemporary design education programmes in India through an analysis of institutional manifestos, mission and vision statements; curriculums and courses; and pedagogic frameworks.

The contemporary design education programmes in India are rooted in the developments of the post-colonial period, challenges of a newly independent nation, industrialisation and adoption of a Western model of progress. With growing promotion of mass production and consumerism, contemporary design education programmes are largely catering to the demands of the market and mainstream industry focused on the economics of consumerism and profit-making. The contemporary curriculum, courses and pedagogic frameworks do not appear to prioritise the social responsibility of designers and are largely oriented towards providing the skills design students need to fulfil the growing demand of the market and industry.

Modern Design Education in India

In 2006, N Cross had explained the place design education occupies in the general education system. He said that the two already-established areas can be broadly classified as education in the sciences and education in the arts, or humanities. These 'two cultures' have long been recognised as dominating our social, cultural and educational systems. The 'third culture' is not so easily recognised, simply because it has been neglected, and has not been adequately named or articulated. In their report (Royal College of Art, 1979), Bruce Archer and his colleagues were prepared to call it 'Design with a capital D.'[1] Design has been a 'minority profession'[2] compared to other mainstream professions that stem from the two already-established areas of education. This identification of design as a minority third culture was largely valid in the Indian context, as it was in other parts of the world.

DOI: 10.4324/9781003383352-6

M. P. Ranjan, an internationally acclaimed design thinker and professor of design at National Institute of Design (NID) for over 40 years, describes the roots of modern design education thus:

> Modern design education had its roots in the Industrial Revolution when changing modes of production displaced existing crafts traditions and apprenticeship processes... The Bauhaus in Germany was the first school... to prepare new students to enter a journey of design learning. Set up in 1919 after the end of the First World War... the educational experiments of the school still find an echo in all design education across the globe... The work that was started in the Bauhaus continued unabated after the teachers were dispersed to new locations by the upheavals in Europe that led to its closure.[3]

Ranjan points to the displacement of existing craft traditions and the erosion of traditional methods of family-based training and apprenticeship processes and associated values. This took place due to large-scale industrialisation and mechanised production. The World Wars and the rebuilding processes, and changes in societal values and aspirations, brought up new issues, challenges and debates in the context of design and design education both in the West and the East.

In her doctoral research, Suchitra Balasubrahmanyan explores the 19th-century debates in India and Britain on art, craft, industrialisation and mechanisation of production that brought forth many dyads: man and machine, utility and ornament, East and West, aesthetics and economics. She highlighted the emergence of 'design' as a distinct epistemological category unifying these seemingly irreconcilable dyads by bringing together the "separate realms of art and manufacturing with the mission of improving, at once, the aesthetics and utility of machine-made products, improving profits and public taste, bridging East and West and humanizing the machine."[4]

Development of modern design education in India had conceptual links to the new centres for training in the 'practical arts' or 'industrial arts' that had emerged in Britain, which were re-christened 'Schools of Design,' to address the exigencies of industrialisation. According to Balasubrahmanyan, design was a "transplant in colonial India through arts schools established in that period."[5] They were initially established in four major cities—Bombay, Madras, Calcutta and Lahore. Sir Jamsetjee Jeejeebhoy School of Art (generally known as the JJ School) was established in Bombay in 1857. By the end of the 19th century, similar institutions were also set up in places like Baroda, Hyderabad, Jaipur and Alwar.[6] Balasubrahmanyan points out that these institutions carried names such as School of Art, School of Industrial Art or School of Industrial Arts and Crafts. Nomenclature like 'School of Design' did not appear, even when there was direct influence of the British schools of design on these institutions. In many ways, these art schools paved the path to the development of design education in India. They provided the workforce for applied arts in the field of industrial art and commercial art. Many individuals who took responsibility for design education in India received their own education in these art schools. However,

> the genesis of institutions for design education in India took place only in the mid-twentieth century. Yet, this development was conceptually and operationally linked to events and debates which took place on the issue of art and industry over the preceding hundred years in Britain and subsequently in India.[7]

In this context, it will be relevant to discuss the engendering of the Arts and Crafts Movement that originated in Britain around 1880s.[8] It

> originated as an aesthetic reaction against the decorative idiom of machine-produced goods, which were ornate, insensitive to the qualities of the materials used and which sacrificed utility in order to appeal to the affluent middle-class's insatiable hunger for novelty and variety.[9]

The moral, social, cultural, ethical, aesthetical and political values of the movement had a global appeal and continue to resonate even today.

William Morris, an influential thinker of the Arts and Crafts Movement, described the debasement of the values associated with craft—in favour of commerce, industrialisation and market economy—as 'sickness of the civilisation.' He drew attention to, and put forward his concerns regarding, the spread of this 'sickness' to the East. In the context of the arts and crafts heritage of India, Morris points out:

> ...an art at once beautiful, orderly, living in our own day, and above all, popular. Now, it is a grievous result of the sickness of civilization that this art is fast disappearing before the advance of western conquest and commerce–fast, and everyday faster... Englishmen in India are, in their short-sightedness, actively destroying the very sources of that education—jewellery, metal-work, pottery, calico-printing, brocade-weaving, carpet-making—all the famous and historical arts of the great peninsula have been for long treated as matters of no importance, to be thrust aside for the advantage of any paltry scrap of so-called commerce; and matters are now speedily coming to an end there.[10]

To understand the genesis of modern design education in India, it is relevant to delve into the process of rebuilding and reconstituting post-colonial India (liberated from the British rule in 1947) and the development dilemmas faced by the architects of modern India. Under the influence of the colonial rulers, India, with its well-established base of craft traditions, was already experiencing transformational impacts of industrialisation and mechanised mass production. Indian influential thinkers such as Rabindranath Tagore, Anand Coomaraswami and M. K. Gandhi articulated a vision of modern India where the past was seen as a resource for building the future unlike the vision of the industrialists and economists for whom prosperity could be achieved only by distancing India from her past.

As the first prime minister of independent India, Jawaharlal Lal Nehru envisioned a self-reliant India and good living standards for the citizens. Nehru was well aware of the ideas and ideals of Gandhi, Tagore and others. However, Nehru was highly influenced by the notion of scientific and technological mediation in the 'progress' models of industrialisation in the developed and developing nations. He believed that village industries could never provide even the essential material and cultural goods that we need today. And they cannot compete with the machine. Nehru asked: "Is it desirable or possible for us to stop the functioning of big-scale machinery in our country?"[11] Ultimately, Prime Minister Nehru led the economic, social and cultural transformation process of the newly independent nation with his vision of scientific, technological and industrial modernity which overshadowed other alternatives.

Nehru believed that true culture derives its inspiration from every corner of the world but it is home-grown and has to be based on the wide mass of people. Therefore, Nehru was open to assistance and cooperation from outside. In his autobiography, he wrote: "We shall want help of many foreign experts in many departments of public activity, particularly in those which require special technical and scientific knowledge."[12]

According to Balasubrahmanyan, the introduction of design education in India was a "conscious and considered act," i.e., a result of deliberate steps taken by Indian policymakers. When India established formal design education through the formation of NID, the model of development was industrialisation. It was believed that the industrial culture was going to address the issues of 'backwardness' because the colonial masters had believed that India was 'backward' and it was an epithet that the free India wanted to rid itself of. A decade after the nation became independent, the Government of India issued an invitation to eminent American designers, Charles and Ray Eames. They prepared *The India Report* in 1958, which led to the establishment of an NID in Ahmedabad.

Right at the beginning of *The India Report*, Eames & Eames state:

> We have been asked by the Government of India to recommend a program of training in the area of design which would serve as an aid to the small industries. We have been asked to state what India can do to resist the rapid deterioration of consumer goods within the country today.

This can be seen as a brief from the government which the Eames followed in order to prepare their recommendations. The report also outlines the focus of the government as largely being on catalysing industrialisation and production activities of consumer goods.

> Based on the recommendations made in *The India Report*, the Government of India with the assistance of the Ford Foundation and the Sarabhai family established the National Institute of Industrial Design, as it was originally called as [sic] an autonomous all-India body in September 1961 at Ahmedabad.[13]

Later, it was renamed the National Institute of Design (NID).[14] Subsequently, in 1969, Industrial Design Centre (IDC) was established at the Indian Institute of Technology (IIT) in Bombay.

These pioneering design education institutions of the 1960s were strongly influenced by Western models of modern design education as well as the Western ethos of that time. Ashoke Chatterjee, former director of NID, points out that "NID was the first attempt by any developing country to use the design disciplines inherited from the Bauhaus as a tool for national regeneration."[15] The Bauhaus influence on the NID was actually mediated and channelled through the Ulm-NID relationship.[16] In the preface to a 1975 report on the Foundation programme of NID, Chatterjee, who was then the director of the Institute, also refers to the Western influence on NID's education programme: "The experience our teachers had in Basel, Ulm, and in several other design schools in Europe and the United States, were valuable…"[17] Chatterjee reflects further that teachers had very little time to process their own experiences gained from abroad. Faculty members who formed the teaching force at NID and IDC in the initial years, for example, H. Kumar Vyas, Sudhakar Nadkarni, Paramanand Dalwadi, Gajanan Upadhayay, Jayanti Panchal, Mohan Bhandari, S M Shah, Manu Gajjar, Mahendra C. Patel and Kirti Trivedi among others, had close connections with Ulm or Basel in the 1960s and later. In addition to Charles and Ray Eames, several other international visitors and teachers contributed to the education programme and training of trainers in India: for instance, Frei Otto, Hans Gugelot, Arno Votler, Herbert Lindinger, Christian Staub, Wolfgang Siol, Armin Hofman, Rolf Misol and Louis Khan.[18]

The above discussion is illustrative of the influences of the colonial and Western values—ideas of modernisation and development, mechanisation and industrialisation, mass production and consumerism, arts and aesthetics—upon the curriculum and pedagogy of modern design education in India. The emergence of design education in India related to what Jan Michl, in his article titled "A case against the modernist regime in design education," describes as "modernist monopolization of design education" through the spread of the Bauhaus curriculum of the 1920s in the design pedagogy of practically all industrialised countries after the Second World War, leading to an "aesthetically unified" "single-style modernist regime of contemporary design schools."[19]

This effect further trickles down into the contemporary design education programmes in India. In the course of my research, experts, during their interviews, referred to the influence of NID and IDC, as premier institutions of India that significantly influenced all subsequent design education programmes in the country. On the one hand, these institutions served as models for pedagogic and curricular frameworks for new design education initiatives. On the other hand, many NID and IDC graduates took up academic as well as administrative positions and spearheaded design education programmes across the country. Thus, similar to other parts of the world, the modernist monopolisation of design education became characteristic of a significant number of contemporary design institutions in India.

Contemporary Design Education in India

Since the inception of NID in 1961, India has seen an increase in the number of design schools and programmes:

> Indian Institute of Technology (IIT) in Mumbai (1969), Delhi (1985) and Guwahati (1996) started programmes in Industrial design while the NIFT [National Institute of Fashion Technology, New Delhi] expanded its reach by setting up centres in Mumbai, Calcutta, Gandhinagar, Hyderabad, Bangalore and Chennai in rapid succession in the late nineties.[20]

By 2010, NIFT centres spread beyond these metropolises to smaller cities and towns: Bhopal, Bhubaneswar, Jodhpur, Kangra, Kannur, Patna, Raebareli and Shillong. Adding to its earlier design education initiative, the Government of India, in 2013, initiated the process of setting up four new NIDs in Jorhat, Kurukshetra, Vijayawada and Bhopal. With the increasing demand for design professionals, the private sector also joined the business of design education across India. Pearl Academy, founded in 1993 (now with campuses at Delhi, Noida, Mumbai and Jaipur), Srishti Institute of Art, Design and Technology, founded in 1996 in Bangalore, and MIT Institute of Design, Pune, which started its operations in 2006, are a few of the notable private education providers, among others.

It should also be noted that design education opportunities in India attracted international players. Several design schools in India have international accreditation partners. In 2011, Laureate Education, Inc., USA, as part of their Laureate Design Universities, acquired Pearl Academy. In 2013, Parsons New School for Design, USA, partnered with the Indian School of Design and Innovation (ISDI), Mumbai and registered their presence in India. Stanford University's D-School is known to have been in consultative discussions with Ahmedabad University, Ahmedabad.

The exponential increase in the number of various new design education programmes took place through public or private initiatives, or both. These programmes sprang up either as departments in universities or standalone design schools and even small independent design education initiatives. The growing involvement of private businesses, with huge financial investments and collaborations with institutions from outside India, further points to the high and rising demand from aspirants for design education. This could also be linked to increased demands from the industry that at present offers new career opportunities.

Figure 5.1 shows the number of design education programs that have been established since the founding of the NID in 1961. There was a significant increase in the number of programs in the 1990s, around the time of economic liberalisation in India, and exponential growth since then. Between 2006 and 2017, the number of new programs skyrocketed. It is worth noting that the number of seats available for student enrolment in each programme has also rapidly increased in recent years, although this is not reflected in the figure.

Individuals who studied design and/or started practising design in India before the 1990s, during interviews with the author, corroborated the above findings. Many of the respondents stressed that the globalisation and liberalisation of the Indian economy from the 1990s paved the path for their lesser-understood 'minority profession' to develop into a mainstream profession in India.

Kirti Trivedi, former professor of design at IDC, recalls:

> The National Institute of Design (NID) and the Industrial Design Centre (IDC) were established in the 1960s with public money to help in the social and economic development of India. The early student projects in these institutes reflect this concern.[21]

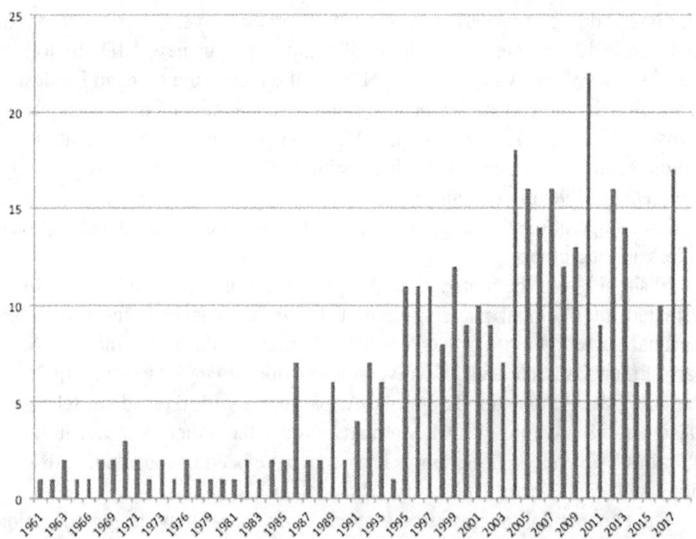

Figure 5.1 Growth of design education in India 1961–2017. Year-wise representation of new design institutions, departments and programmes in India.

He also points out that "with the repositioning of design as a marketing tool in the era following the so-called 'globalisation' of the Indian economy, this perception of the role of design has sharply changed." This change in role, i.e., contemporary developments in Indian design education programmes, will be evaluated in the remainder of the chapter by examining:

- Manifestos, mission and vision statements
- Curriculums and courses
- Pedagogic frameworks

Analysis of Manifestos, Mission and Vision Statements

A study of several design education institutions' manifestos, and mission and vision statements available in the public domain reveals these institutions' intent to foster values of social and cultural relevance and service, address the needs of different sectors, humanise technologies, raise quality of life, promote design awareness, and address the larger local and global problems.

Eames & Eames, in *The India Report*, presented the vision for an NID that

> will hasten the production of the 'Lotas' of our time. By this we mean a hope that an attitude be generated that will appraise and solve the problems of our coming times with the same tremendous service, dignity, and love that the Lota served its time.[22]

The following example of a vision and mission statement from IDC conveys that the institution aspires to deliver:

> A holistic design education that shapes the students into responsible contributors to the society. It enables them to identify significant contemporary problems, inculcate critical thinking, critique conventional solutions, and challenge the status quo to arrive at creative solutions through collaborative team efforts at different levels of society and influencing policymaking that lead to innovations.[23]

Rashmi Korjan, a practising designer with over 33 years' experience, has been associated with more than ten design schools in India during her design career. She points out:

> when NID started, they had *The India Report*. And *The India Report* laid down a whole approach. I think it also had the benefit of being very early post-independence. The whole zeal of building the country, building the nation somehow rubbed off on a lot of institutions from that time—the early IIMs, the early IITs and all.[24]

Korjan further observes that the spirit and fervour have worn out now, leaving a void. She emphasises the importance of a stated mission for fostering organisational culture, so that the organisation can attract the right kind of people who would align with it. However, in her view, mission statements often fail to transpire into the organisational culture to establish what design is and what it could do in the larger social context. Chatterjee expresses a similar concern:

> Indeed, it [social responsibility] was a foundation for introducing the [design] profession to India 50 years ago, and integrated into the curriculum by educators aware of their responsibility. Yes, living up to that promise remains a task. As in many professional disciplines in our land, the gap between promise and delivery remains huge.[25]

In February 2007, the Government of India approved and released the National Design Policy. The policy document highlights the realisation of

> the increasing importance of design in economic, industrial and societal development and in improving the quality of products and services... Strengthening quality design education at different levels is identified as one of the key strategies to achieve the visions of the policy. One of several measures to promote quality design education that were listed in the policy document was the setting up of four national institutes of design in different parts of the country on the pattern of the NID.[26]

A critical examination of the National Design Policy reveals sparse and ritualistic mention of social significance of design. As part of the design framework, the document outlines supporting India's Industrial Policy as one of the primary objectives of the Design Policy. Furthermore, the document places heavy emphasis on the role of design in 'national and industrial competitiveness' in 'manufacturing and service industry' and aims to brand and position 'Indian design within India and overseas, enhancing design and design service exports' as an 'engine of economic and industrial growth."[27]

Concerns related to the formation of new national institutes of design, as articulated in the National Design Policy, sparked a debate on the Internet and social networks among groups of design educators and design professionals. One of the key concerns was the lack of a well-informed and contemporary vision behind the formation of the new national institutes of design:

> We believe this new effort must once again yield institutions that are well-informed and borne out of the most contemporary, bold and forward looking thinking in design. It will be a lost opportunity if we follow a predetermined route and only end up replicating expired, limited and ineffective models of design.[28]

This led to the formation of Vision First—an independent initiative by 'citizen designers'[29]—whose activities peaked in 2011–2012 and involved consultations and brainstorming that led to a proposal presented to the Government of India.

The proposal document of Vision First highlights the need for contemporary design vision in response to the dramatic transformation around the world. The document points out that "design and design thinking are increasingly about building in capabilites [*sic*] that empower and enable people to use these resources, with quality of life and environment as the guiding principles, not just economic factors which are also important."[30] Without denying the importance of the economic factors, the proposal stresses the larger significance of environmental and social values that are empowering and enabling. In congruence with the theory of *wicked problems*, the document elaborates on the significance of design in addressing such problems:

> Around the world design is now being appreciated and put to use as an essential approach in dealing with those problems that have no linear, step-by-step solutions but require a leap of faith towards integrated, radical new answers. This set includes all the issues of our times – poverty, health, food production, unemployment, sustainability, terrorism... the list is long. The old analytical approaches are found wanting in the face of these ill-defined, complex problems. This is possible through design because it works with a different set of processes: repeatedly reframing the problem, engaging with stakeholders, prototyping and testing solutions, exploring alternatives, visioning scenarios and so on.[31]

The fact that a large number of citizen designers came together to raise concerns and debate, seeing it as a part of their responsibility, highlights the significance of a holistic vision and mission. It is also indicative of the prevailing lack of clarity of vision as well as the gravity of this situation. It is yet to be seen whether the government and private players will address the issues raised in the Vision First Proposal or overlook them as contemporary design education continues to develop.

Another observation, articulated by several interviewed experts, concerns the trend to present well-worded vision and mission statements with some kind of a social mandate on the websites of design education programmes and institutes. However, most respondents were of the opinion that, most often, these statements are mere examples of pompous rhetoric without definite implementation plans or actionable components in place.

Korjan is of the view that if an institutional vision is to be rolled out as an integral part of the programme, it has to be spoken about; it needs to be something that the entire faculty is aware of, something that students, staff and everyone involved in the education programme encounters and imbibes.

It has to be a common agenda. However, she observes that manifestos and vision statements remain confined to a file or a document which is tucked away. Many a time, only some founding members of the institution are aware of the existence of such vision documents. At most, these statements may take the form of slogans and become part of promotional propaganda. They do not really manifest within the actual education programme. Korjan elaborates on her observations: "whenever I am invited to teach, I am never given that statement, I am never told that: okay, this is what we stand for, this is our vision statement."[32]

In summary, the following significant points emerged from the study of manifestos, mission and vision statements:

- Concerns for social and ethical values, environmental issues, raising the quality of living, service to humanity and other aspects of social responsibility are accentuated in some form in the majority of mission and vision statements put forward by design education institutions.
- There is a lack of thrust in making the institutional vision statement fundamental to all the activities of that institution.
- There is a lack of clarity regarding actionable processes for achieving the promises that are articulated in institutional mission and vision statements.
- There are no recommendations or indications of assessment processes for institutional accountability and progress audit for advancement towards the achievement of institutional vision, mission and promises made through manifestos.
- Focus on social responsibility is lacking in the mandate and vision for design education, as articulated in India's National Design Policy.

Analysis of Curriculums and Course Outlines

To actualise the promise that is presented to the society by an educational institution through its mandate, mission and vision statements, first and foremost the institution requires a curriculum and courses that represent, resonate, reflect and reinforce the original intent.

The interviewed experts held concurring views while responding to the query regarding institutional statements. They highlighted a wide gap between the intent and actualisation of fostering values of social responsibility and larger public good. Most of them opined that there were few opportunities within the curriculum to address issues related to social responsibility values and related institutional mandates. In comparison, they noted that the major curricular emphasis is on skills-oriented courses that aligned with the expectations and demands of the industry and job market by focusing on the transfer of skills and techniques; know-how of tools and technology; and client presentation techniques to sell ideas, concepts, products and services. The experts viewed that such courses made up 85%–90% of the total course offerings.

Study and analysis of curriculum/syllabus/semester flowcharts of several contemporary design education programmes support these observations. In the foundation year of design education programmes, skills-oriented courses accounted for between 80% and 84% of the time allocation. Courses which could be connected to aspects of social responsibility and environmental concerns and which could possibly contribute to the development of such understanding ranged between 16% and 20%. In the following years of specialisation, the latter percentage reduced to 5%–6% of the total time allocation and comprised mostly non-core peripheral courses, while the central focus remained on the specialisation of specific skills, technical inputs for know-how, presentation techniques, exposure and understanding of the industry, and professional projects and practices, for better employability. It can well be argued that without a proper foundation of skills, these design students cannot aspire to assume the role of employable design professionals in future. However, an array of skills without the conceptual understanding of the wider interconnections and responsibilities of a powerful profession is akin to putting firearms into amateur hands.

A. Balasubramaniam, a design practitioner with 31 years of experience, has been associated with several design schools as a visiting academic or as a member of their advisory bodies for 21 years. He observes that most of the contemporary design education programmes are employability driven, training students in the "craft of design," i.e., supplying graduates who have strong software skills, are meticulous with getting the forms and the kerning right, can deliver sophisticated-looking, polished output, but who are not thinking individuals. He describes them as "Photoshop donkeys"[33] and explains: "Because they are good, they don't think. And design is essentially a thinking profession that relies on soft skills—on sensitivity, team work, being grounded, developing empathy."[34] Such soft skills would be essential to deal with the social and cultural *wicked problems* and larger challenges that designers in India need to address.

The focus of curriculums is mainly on specific networks of production and consumption which are only one part of the 'model of contemporary networks' described in the previous chapter. A close examination of the contemporary design education programmes highlights the fact that most of these programmes are primarily geared towards providing training to students so that they become employable design professionals in order to meet the projected needs of the market and the industry. "Like so much of education, design learning has become big business and design schools are in danger of becoming facility centres rather than spaces for value-based systems."[35]

Referring to organisations like the India Design Council,[36] Balasubramaniam points out that it is the job of such organisations to ensure that both design education and the design profession address the diverse design needs and *wicked problems* faced by the masses in a country like India. But he does not see that happening. He points out that since most of these bodies largely consist of industry stalwarts, "they think design is an industry. So, we are creating 'Photoshop donkeys' because the industry wants them. They don't want thinking individuals. They want somebody who will when they say do this, they will do it."[37]

The claims raised by Balasubramaniam are further supported by reviewing the India Design Council's list of its major intended activities related to design education:

- Benchmark design institutions.
- Develop and design standardised design syllabi for all institutions imparting design education in India.
- Encourage close cooperation between academia and industry to produce proprietary design know-how while encouraging creation of new design-led enterprises for wealth creation.
- Assist industries to engage the services of designers for their existing and new products.
- Alongside these activities, the Council emphasises facilitating a culture of creating and protecting intellectual property in the area of design, encouraging design and design-led exports including undertaking design work outsourced by other countries; and enhancing country's international competitiveness. The intended activities of the India Design Council reinforce the industry perspective—its development, profitability and growth—in the conceptual framework of design education. There is no significant mention of directing design education towards social relevance and addressing larger developmental issues and problems. Development of standardised syllabi and curriculums with skewed vision cannot result in holistic and balanced design education programmes that can uphold and induce social responsibility values. Moreover, standardisation may not adequately support the diverse needs of the population and address varied *wicked problems* in a vast country like India. Such short-sighted standardisation would undermine the larger potential of social relevance of design and miss an opportunity to induce related values in the students.

To sum up, the analysis of curriculums and courses in relation to social responsibility values resulted in providing the following key insights:

- The curriculums are largely focused on teaching design graduates to fulfil the needs and demands of the industry.
- Social responsibility and related values hold little significance within the examined curriculums.
- The philosophical and conceptual intent of socially responsible design—as expressed in institutional manifestos, vision and mission statements—does not seem to faithfully translate into the curriculums of the examined design education programmes.

- The gap between visualisation and actualisation poses a major challenge in consistently incorporating, fostering and implementing social responsibility values as significant programme goals.
- Although social responsibility values are accorded low priority in the curricular structures of most design education programmes, these programmes are not completely devoid of such values.

Analysis of Pedagogic Frameworks

Conceptually, a pedagogic framework can be seen as the vital component that activates the circuit consisting of an institutional manifesto and vision and mission statement on the one hand, and of the curriculum and courses in a given education programme on the other. I now examine the teaching methods and practices prevalent in design education programmes in India to analyse the components within the pedagogic frameworks that contribute to fostering values of social responsibility.

The contemporary pedagogic frameworks of design education in India remain largely rooted in the 'modernist regime of design education' that stems from the Bauhaus approach. In response to how the focus of contemporary design education programmes—in the context of their curricular focus and pedagogic frameworks—has changed over the last ten years compared to the earlier period, almost all respondents expressed that they do not see any major change. Suchitra Balasubrahmanyan, an NID alumna and a professional designer with 25 years of experience who has been involved in design education research and design education for 19 years, explains: "It is not as if design education has not changed. But, I do not see a big shift or any basic enquiry, which moves away from that Bauhaus mode of teaching, no radical change." She further elaborates:

> From five and a half years, the programme at the NID has been trimmed to four years. I feel the packaging may have changed; the title or labelling [of courses] may have changed; new courses have started, like, new media and user interface. But I do not think the premise of design education has changed or has been radically re-examined.[38]

S. Balaram, in his article 'Design Pedagogy in India: A Perspective,' points out: "India in its characteristic way particularly assimilated the *Vorkurs* or preliminary course of the Bauhaus."[39] To outline the pedagogic structure of a design education programme in India, Balaram adds: "Although generalization is difficult, the typical program starts with skill learning as the basic design course, and proceeds to application in projects, which progressively grow in their complexity and include technical as well as conceptual integration." A programme leading to a bachelor's degree or equivalent usually spans over four years. The first year is a general (not discipline-specific) foundation year with preliminary courses. After this, students take up a specific discipline of specialisation. During the initial semesters in specific disciplines students acquire basic skills related to the area of specialisation. Instruction usually proceeds in the form of projects, moving from the simple ones to those of increasing complexity. "Much of the design education in India is project-based; students are encouraged to take an empirical, intuitive approach to design problems and to experiment freely with new forms, new materials and processes, and to develop original, creative thinking."[40] These projects could be hypothetical or real-life projects with real clients. Towards the first part of the final year, students take an internship related to a specific area of specialisation, to gain production or industrial experience, or experience of working at a professional design studio.

> Only after this are the students allowed to proceed to the final project or thesis, where they are expected to demonstrate an acceptable level of professional competence. The curriculum emphasizes project learning, in which production situation and professional practice situation are considered tools of learning.

He further claims that 'learning by doing' refined to 'learning to know and learning to do' became the credo of design education in India with the realisation that it is more important 'to make one learn' than to teach one. "Within this broad principle, teaching methods vary greatly around the country. The most prevailing ones are studio work, individual guidance and group discussion. Lecturing and textbook reading are kept to a minimum." For most courses, there are no prescribed textbooks but a suggested reading list. The 'read and write' pedagogical approach is commonly abandoned in favour of a 'show and tell' process of demonstrating what has been achieved during a project through presentations by the "self-directed learner, group discussions and just-in-time guidance from facilitator."[41]

Evaluation of students' progress is a requirement of any education programme. This process has largely been qualitative in nature, which reflects the nature of design and design education. Periodic feedback from the facilitator during project work is followed by an overall evaluation at the end of the course. Semester-end evaluation by a panel of academic members has been the common practice. Due to growing student numbers and the need to benchmark against other education providers, some design education programmes have introduced quantitative assessment models or a mix of qualitative and quantitative evaluation processes. Social responsibility values incorporated in a project are missing from most assessment rubrics or do not constitute an essential part of the evaluation criteria, which is a notable finding. The values of social responsibility are usually seen as an additional or optional quality of a design outcome and are thus not represented in its assessment criteria.

A facilitator, in the role of a project guide, advisor, motivator and evaluator, is comparable but quite different when compared to a teacher in the conventional sense. The pedagogic methods of design education in India are also quite different from the pedagogic methods of conventional secondary schooling, where the stress is on memorisation and recall, which allows little space for self-direction. Consequently, students need significant re-orientation to the kind of teaching/guidance they encounter upon joining a design education programme at the bachelor's degree level.

At the master's degree level, the pedagogic methods remain more or less similar to those used in undergraduate degrees. However, the programme duration is shorter, usually between two and two and a half years. There is only discipline-specific shorter duration of foundational inputs as compared to a longer and more general foundation programme at the bachelor's degree level. Other courses are also condensed in time duration and coverage of assignments.

Professional education in design involves both the teaching of design-related knowledge and skills, as well as practice under supervision. The teachers who impart such education, thus are required to be practising professionals. Different design institutions in India have different policies and norms regarding the private practice options of full-time faculty members. However, to expose the students to a larger variety of professional practice insights, experts from the industry and design professionals are invited as visiting faculties and guest faculty.

Several of the interviewed experts who have headed design schools or programmes report difficulty in recruiting enough full-time faculty, which is a significant reason for inviting many visiting faculty members. The interviewees indicated that at many design schools visiting faculty makes up 60%–70% of the teaching force, if not more. A small number of permanent full-time faculty members in positions of power within the institution make decisions about which course would be on the timetable and which one would be cancelled, which visiting faculty would be invited and so on. However, the pedagogic delivery is heavily dependent on the visiting faculty. The visiting faculty and even permanent staff may or may not be attuned to the larger vision and mission of the institution or the overarching curricular goals. I. S. Mathur (2014),[42] in his concluding editorial remarks in the book *Design Education in India: Retrospection, Introspection, and Perception*, claims:

> Every institution starts its academic programme with a certain set of objectives and mandates but when new faculty members join in, they try to change the course contents and this is not in tune with the original mandate… this entire process can become extremely subjective and deviate from the norms of institutional culture.

These remarks highlight the flexibility of delivery—the ease with which changes can be made to the course content and, therefore, the pedagogy associated with it. New faculty members (including visiting academics) may not be intentionally attempting to change courses so as to dissociate them from the institutional mission and mandate. A new faculty member or visiting faculty, as discussed earlier, may not even be briefed about the institutional manifesto, vision and mission. Assuming that changes are not frivolous, it is possible that they are necessary and well justified or simply need further investigation/consideration.

Jatin Bhatt, a design practitioner with 45 years of experience and a design educator for 25 years, has advised and headed various design education programmes and institutions. Bhatt mentioned another dimension to this issue: Design education institutions look for faculty members who are not run-of-the-mill but are mavericks and disruptive. Such individuals are perceived to be of huge value to design pedagogy, even though dealing with such kind of people could hold many challenges for the institutions unless the leadership is visionary and willing to deal with them. However, it is this kind of individual amongst the faculty members that, in Bhatt's view, "in a way creates multiple dialogues or multiple directions or more perspectives on design." Bhatt goes on to warn that "it may create havoc in the mind of a young student, confuse the person, but I think within 3–4 years they find their alignment. But institutional roles should be to open up these multiple avenues."[43]

With regard to the contemporary design students at the receiving end of the pedagogic explorations by individual faculty members, the interviewed experts pointed to significant paradigm shifts that have happened with young learners today. They are of the opinion that, among others, such changes are largely induced by socio-economic factors. Over the years, the monetary investments in getting design education have multiplied manifold. On the one hand, there are economic pressures like repaying student loans, or quick returns on 'investments' made in acquiring the diploma or degree. On the other hand, there are aspirations of meeting the prevalent social norms of 'success' and 'good life.' Lucrative offers and glamour of the mainstream industry present tough choices to young designers to opt for less remuneration and more challenging paths of carrying forward the social responsibility agenda. However, the experts are of the opinion that these challenges have not been proportionally reciprocated as changes in the pedagogy and programme approach. Against the backdrop of his decades of experience with design education, Bhatt observes:

> The change actually has come about from the perspective of the aspiration of the students who apply for design preparation. And that, in a way, defines change. Because aspirations are different, the quality and nature of engagement are different. And the purpose for which people now and through which students engage with design education is different. So, in

a way, while contents and curricula haven't gone through a major change, there is a major change in terms of the way in which students engage with education. To me, that's a major shift and that also calls for really looking at design education very differently.[44]

The findings from the analysis of the pedagogic frameworks of design education in India can be summarised as follows:

- The contemporary pedagogic framework largely carries forward the legacy of the 'modernist regime of design education' without any significant, radical adjustment to address the fast-paced changes in the contemporary world.
- The pedagogical framework is reflective of the curriculum; therefore, something missing in the curriculum can lead to its absence in course delivery.
- Personal beliefs and worldviews of individual faculty members significantly influence the pedagogical methods they opt to use during course delivery.
- There appear to be no clear, specific pedagogical techniques or components that would work towards fostering values of social responsibility or develop understanding to address larger issues and dimensions of *wicked problems*.
- Modifications of the curriculum can lead to a more conducive pedagogic framework, where both faculty members and students can be oriented to bring in specific emphasis on the values of social responsibility and related issues.

The research shows that social responsibility is valued but only 'on paper' at the level of institutional mission and vision statements. In contrast to any officially declared intents, the curricular foci, courses, pedagogic frameworks and assessment and evaluation processes do not appear to be conducive to fostering social responsibility values in design students.

Notes

1 Cross, N. *Designerly Ways of Knowing*. London: Springer, 2006.

2 Potter, N. *What Is a Designer: Things, Places, Messages* (2nd ed.). London: Hyphen Press, 1980 described the profession of designers as "minority profession." p.13.

3 Ranjan, M. P. Lessons from Bauhaus, Ulm and NID: Role of Basic Design in Postgraduate Education. In V. S. Katiyar & S. Mehta (Eds.) *Design Educations—Tradition and Modernity: Scholistic Papers from the International Conference, DETM 05.2005* (pp.2–9). Ahmedabad: NID.

4 Balasubrahmanyan, S. *Genesis of Design Education in India: The Warp and Weft of Local – Global Contexts* (Diss). Ahmedabad: CEPT University, 2012. p.38.

5 Ibid., p.vi.

6 Dutta, A. *The Bureaucracy of Beauty: Design in the Age of Its Global Reproductibility*. New York: Routledge, 2007. p.27.

7 Balasubrahmanyan, S. Op cit. p.16.
8 John Ruskin, William Morris and Charles Robert Ashbee were some of the influential contributors to the Arts and Crafts Movement.
9 Balasubrahmanyan, S. Op cit. p.39.
10 Kelvin, N. *William Morris on Art and Socialism*. The Minneola, NY: Dover Publications, 1999. p.24.
11 Nehru, J. *The Discovery of India* (Century edition). Delhi: Oxford University Press, 1989. p.526.
12 Nehru, J. *An Autobiography*. New Delhi: Oxford University Press, 1985. p.445.
13 National Institute of Design-History and Background. 2015. Retrieved from http://www.nid.edu/about/history-of-nid.
14 Adrian Frutiger, the renowned Swiss graphic designer, created the NID symbol in mid-1960s.
15 Chatterjee, A. *Design for Change; Five Decades of an Indian Challenge in Awareness and Education*. Lecture Presented at the MN Buch Memorial Lecture, Bhopal, 2015.
16 In 2010, two conferences titled "Look Back, Look Forward" were organised in Bengaluru and Kolkata to investigate the links and influences of HfG Ulm and design education in India.
17 National Institute of Design. *50 Years of the National Institute of Design 1961–2011*. Ahmedabad: NID.
18 Ranjan, M. P. Design for India: Web of Connections: Indian Design Education with Influences from the HfG Ulm. Retrieved from http://design-for-india.blogspot.com.2013/01/recognising-roots-nid-accorded-status.html.
19 Michl, J. A Case against the Modernist Regime in Design Education. Retrieved 27 June 2012 from http://www.janmichl.com/english-only.html.
20 Ranjan, M. P. The Avalanche Effect: Institutional frameworks and design as a development resource in India. Privately published 2002.
21 Trivedi, K. Sarvodaya-Betterment of All. *ICSID News*, February 2003.
22 Eames, C., & Eames, R. 1991, Op cit., p.66.
23 Industrial Design Centre (IDC), IIT Bombay; Vision and Mission. Retrieved from https://www.idc.iitb.ac.in/abouts/vision-mission
24 Korjan, R., personal communication with the author, 21 July 2016.
25 Chatterjee, A., personal communication with the author, 13 July 2016.
26 National Design Policy Approved by the Government of India, 2011.
27 Ibid., pp.5–7.
28 Vision First-Proposal. (2011, February 11). Retrieved from https://visionpehle.wordpress.com/proposal/.
29 This term draws upon the title of the book *Citizen Designer: Perspectives on Design Responsibility* which attempts to answer: "What does it mean to be a designer in today's corporate-driven, overbranded global consumer culture?" through more than 70 debate-stirring essays and interviews (Heller and Vienne, 2003).
30 Vision First-Proposal. (2011, February 11). Retrieved from https://visionpehle.wordpress.com/proposal.
31 Ibid.
32 Korjan, R., Op cit.
33 Photoshop is a proprietary name of a software package for digital editing and manipulation of photographs and images. Photoshop, launched in the 1990s, has developed into an industry standard and allows complex work with images. The expected proficiency in handling the software and its usage have penetrated so deeply amongst industry professionals, design students and novice amateurs that *photoshop* is also commonly used as a verb now. The industry is known to have a continuous supply of highly proficient Photoshop buffs who do not seem to know what to do with their skills unless told what to do with the software or where to apply it.

34 Balasubramaniam, A., personal communication, 15 July 2016.
35 Chatterjee, A. 2015. Op cit.
36 The India Design Council is a government appointed body. It falls under the auspices of the Department of Industrial Policy and Promotion (DIPP) and has been constituted in pursuance of the National Design Policy announced by the Government of India on 8 February 2007. "Its mission is to promote design awareness and effectiveness of Indian design both within India as well as abroad. While the central aim of the India Design Council is to provide a platform for Indian design to enhance its competitiveness on the global stage, secondary aims include playing an important role in fostering closer ties between industry and academia, and showcasing India's design capabilities" ('National Design Policy,' 2011, p.14).
37 Balasubramaniam, A. Op cit.
38 Balasubrahmanyan, S., personal communication, 18 July 2016.
39 Balaram, S. Design Pedagogy in India: A Perspective. *Design Issues*, 21.4 (2005): pp.11–22. www. jstor.org/stable/25224015.
40 Ibid., p.17.
41 De Parker, I. (Ed.) (2013). Reflecting on the Future of Design Education in 21st Century India: Towards a Paradigm Shift in Design Foundation. In *Teaching Design Foundation & Fundamentals of Design* (pp.26–37). Pune: India Design Council. https://doi.org/10.1007/978-81-322-1050-4_93.
42 Mathur, I. S. *Design Education in India: Retrospection, Introspection, and Perception.* Ahmedabad: NID, 2014.
43 Bhatt, J., personal communication, 18 July 2016.
44 Ibid.

6 Challenges in Imparting Values of Social Responsibility

We now examine the pedagogic issues and practical challenges faced by faculty members and students, undertaking programmes to foster the values of social responsibility. These issues are delineated by three case studies: development of a new design education programme at the Ambedkar University in Delhi and two courses—Environmental Perception (EP) and Design Concepts and Concerns (DCC)—which were particularly referred to by several experts during their interviews. For these two courses, I was one of the resource persons.

The Ambedkar University's School of Design is a case of a nascent but significant re-examination and re-definition of contemporary design education programmes for fostering responsible design values and addressing the complex issues and *wicked problems* faced by the society.

While my research, as well as my experience as faculty, showed that it is not that courses that can foster social responsibility are completely nonexistent; rather, it is that there is not enough emphasis on the impact of commercialisation of design education. The analysis of curriculums, courses and pedagogic frameworks reveals that a few courses appear to have the potential to foster values of social responsibility amongst students. The case studies of EP and DCC illustrate that courses with a potential for fostering values of social responsibility do exist.

Design Education for Social Responsibility

In a typical design project—the input 'problem' is seen as a given, as a client brief, or as a project brief, whether in praxis or in a classroom. The design process starts only after receiving this brief. The output is seen as an outcome of this design 'action' process. However, the designer is not just an outsider acting upon the social system, he is simultaneously an insider acting within the social system and influenced by it. While designing, a creator-designer is acting upon the society from within. In effect, 'serving society' and 'shaping society' can be seen as two sides of the same coin. The intention behind serving and shaping essentially makes the difference. Findeli agrees and has said

DOI: 10.4324/9781003383352-7

that a design project is: "ready to live a life of its own, in another realm. But, in reality, problem and action dwell in the same world, of which the designer is also part, not only as a professional, but also as a citizen."[1] This entails socially responsible design action on the part of the designers in the roles played by them.

It is necessary to consider social responsibility as a broadly inclusive term and not limited to responsibility only to human society because of the highly interconnected and interdependent nature of all the components of the contemporary networks on which the future of the human society depends. Even if humans were absent, nature would continue on its course. However, in disrupting 'nature' from its vital and delicate balance, the human species will probably get wiped out from the face of this planet. Tony Fry, a design theorist with interest in sustainability, creative industries and culture, expresses similar concerns in his book titled *Becoming Human by Design*:

> Such thinking begins with a sober assessment of what we need 'to be' (in order to continue to be) this based upon understanding how ontologically we become what we currently and plurally are. Unevenly, mostly unconsciously, we are at a moment wherein we cannot stay as we were or are but as yet cannot see (at worst) the need or (at best), with any clarity, what it is we have to become and how to become it.[2]

More than ever before, it is vital for contemporary design education programmes to underpin the complexities of socially responsible design beyond the typical education for would-be designers in terms of servicing the client/producer and consumer. The other components of the contemporary network—governance, environment, society, and individual designer—also call for serious considerations and contextual inputs in a design education programme oriented towards responsible design values.

Several experts referred to the developments at the School of Design at the Ambedkar University, Delhi (AUD), as a case which presents an alternate perspective to the on-going trends in most of the contemporary design education programmes in India. Arvind Lodaya, who has 28 years of experience as a practising design professional and has been associated with design education programmes for 15 years, describes the institution

> as a kind of new age institution which has in a sense given itself an old age mandate. It is not talking market; it is not talking technology; it is not talking future and utopian sci-fi kind of scenarios and all that. It is talking masses; it is talking empowerment; it is talking social kind of input and so on.[3]

Following is the case of the School of Design—its manifesto, curricular emphasis and pedagogic framework—that enables us to examine the development of a new direction in contemporary design education.

Case Study 1: School of Design, Ambedkar University, Delhi

Ambedkar University was established in 2007 by the Government of Delhi as a public university offering research, postgraduate and undergraduate programmes in the social sciences and the humanities.[4] The University is named after Dr. B. R. Ambedkar,[5] a visionary Indian social reformer, who is well known for championing the cause of equity, social justice, and rights of women and less privileged groups in society. The vision and mission statement given on the website of the University states:

> The University strongly believes that no knowledge becomes socially productive unless it spreads across society, transcending barriers of caste, creed and class. Only then can teaching and learning become liberating undertakings, contributing to the promotion of equality, social justice and excellence… The University aspires to mould its students into informed and sensitive professionals who will engage with their social responsibilities and will react to the needs of… our society.[6]

This manifesto guided the envisioning of the School of Design, which was established in 2013, as one of the ten schools on the University's plan. It started with three faculty members and currently has seven full-time faculty members. The first academic programme MDes (Social Design) was offered in July 2013 as a Masters in Social Design. It is a two- and half-year full-time programme. Twelve students joined the programme in the first batch. In 2014, 13 students, in 2015, 14 students, and in 2016, 18 students joined the Masters in Social Design programme. The first batch graduated in 2016.

AUD's website highlights the distinctiveness of its School of Design, by introducing this way:

> The School of Design (SDes) at AUD is unique in its conception—this is the first time in India that design education will be institutionally embedded in and collaborating with the humanities and social sciences. The School draws from its distinct position within a Humanities and Social Sciences University to amalgamate core attributes of design with socially complex issues, needs and sectors. By relocating the object-centred design focus to that of the 'social', the School of Design proposes to create better informed, sensitised, empowered and robust communities through new products, services, systems, interfaces and scenarios. This setting offers an opportunity to re-visualise design education and practice in order to creatively meet the multiple challenges offered by a rapidly changing, deeply interconnected local and global landscape. Simultaneously, the School of Design seeks to further, through design, AUD's mandate of creating an equitable, just and sustainable society through social action.[7]

The statement of intent highlights re-visualising design education to address emerging challenges and larger social concerns. The philosophy behind the School of Design at AUD, and its institutional location in the humanities and social sciences setting, sets it apart from other design schools and design departments in other universities. This significantly reinforces the possibility of the actualisation of its intent. Suchitra Balasubrahmanyan, a senior faculty member at the School of Design, points out: the stand-alone design schools are just in and of themselves. They may have a few social science people in the background, for example, the Science and Liberal Arts studies at NID, but their contribution to the curriculum is quite small since they do not really participate in design studios or teaching design courses. The focus of design departments located in technical or engineering institutions, like IITs, is primarily technology. "There is a small humanities component, but it's really quite negligible. They don't make any real impact as such in terms of bringing up big social science thinking." In Balasubrahmanyan's view, the School of Design is perhaps the only institution where the design faculty would have colleagues from the social sciences and humanities as well. She further highlights and emphasises that since the University is named after Ambedkar, the philosophy and ideas of social justice and equity are quite strongly held up at the School.[8]

To further the institutional mandate, the social focus is predominant in the School's curriculum, courses and pedagogic framework as well. The Masters in Social Design (MDes) is a full-time practice and research-based programme:

> It amalgamates methods, tools and approaches of design disciplines with those of social sciences to creatively address complex issues of inclusion, access, equity and opportunities through participatory and co-creation processes. More specifically, the programme aims to address complex design areas of public services, public systems, governance interfaces, community networks pertaining to health, hygiene, education, gender, mobility, waste management, resource access/conservation/distribution (water, electricity etc.), urban and rural commons, internet and digital access, safety, informal economies and such areas. The emphasis of the programme is on preparing students with entrepreneurial competence and leadership essential to addressing socially complex issues embedded in communities, agencies, organisations and the state.[9]

This excerpt from the MDes programme document highlights the focus on preparing students to address complex social issues and stresses it by enlisting several of such areas of concern. The complexity of problems and concerns, resonate with the *wicked problems* and its theory discussed earlier. The offered courses strongly align with the institutional vision and curricular emphasis. The projects taken up by the students further reinforce the spirit of the programme.

Jatin Bhatt, Dean of the School of Design, is of the view that the MSDes programme and the nature of the projects undertaken by the students have fostered a certain set of values, a framework for the School and relative reference for envisioning future programmes. He is of the opinion that, regardless of how much one explains social design, people would want to see its validity and application. And this can only be demonstrated or showcased by the nature of projects that the students undertake. Bhatt enumerates a few such projects undertaken by his students, including: A public health project in Uttar Pradesh, where the students spent three months in a village during their last project; a design project on urban farming; a project on internet privacy; and issues surrounding the Delhi Metro and what can be done to improve it. Referring to a student's project on e-waste management, Bhatt points out to the significance of the perspective from which a student looks at an issue. He explains that the students worked on a system design where the unorganised rag-pickers could be brought into mainstream of the waste management system. However, the students overarching concerns in the project were regarding the ill effects and health hazards related to this work and how dignity, respect and pride, with policy intervention, could be integrated with health management support in designing the waste management system.[10]

Through some of these examples of students' projects, Bhatt emphasises that the brilliance of design is not limited to objects and products. Design can be applied to situations which are more complex in terms of services, processes and systems. Bhatt further illustrates this in the context of effective implementation of government policy:

> Very often, we find that a lot of thought and application of mind and expertise goes into some of the policies that the government formulates. But where it fails is that it just hasn't been thought through in terms of how it is to be delivered.

Bhatt stresses that thinking through and detailing the delivery process is also a part of design. This process can be collaborative and bring in perspectives of people—the real beneficiaries—into the context of public health, access to energy or water and so on. However, since design looks at issues very differently, this process of policy implementation through design can also be disruptive.[11] Bhatt points out that there could be objects and products involved as well. However, he questions: why is it necessary to have everybody who has all that expertise; one could collaborate with others who are already experts in those areas. Thus, Bhatt justifies the stand of the MSDes programme of not teaching conventional design courses predominant in most of the contemporary design education programmes. He further asserts: "We are almost kind of abandoning this traditional skill base in design. Because we believe that [a certain kind of] design can be beyond skills. So that is the major shift in terms of how we are approaching design."[12]

Balasubrahmanyan elaborates: "the Masters programme is open to people from many disciplines and it is trying to focus on a certain practice of design which is perhaps not materially oriented." This is the reason for not including certain traditional skill base. If it were for undergraduates, some of these skill bases might be retained. She goes on to emphasise the need for pedagogical innovation through an example of redefining 'drawing' as a skill.

> It might also change the expectation we have of a designer, as someone who is doing these fabulous drawings. Because let's not forget that many fabulous drawings can be quite empty of thought, insight, sensibility and so on. Therefore, it's not an end in itself.[13]

When the thought and larger social intent behind design action becomes paramount in a programme, like that of the School of Design, it transcends the conventional boundaries of materiality and skills.

Bhatt maintains that it is not for the sake of being disruptive, or just for its newness, that the programme's emphasis has an unconventional curricular approach. The kind of projects the students opt for is evidence for the fact that it is for the sake of more purposeful and meaningful manifestation of design and has space for new stories in design. However, all this is not without struggle and challenges of developing the teaching materials for such a new programme, along with weaving in new insights and learning as the programme develops.[14]

Students for the Masters in Social Design programme have diverse backgrounds for their graduate studies, such as political science, sociology, philosophy, literature, history, information technology, computer programmes and architecture. Bhatt points out that most of them do not have a design perspective. Then, again, the assumption is that this diversity would add value to the programme. However, the faculty members find that while this lends some advantages, it also poses several pedagogic challenges as well as concerns for future prospects of the students.

Mohammad Sharique Farooqui, another senior faculty member at the School of Design, expressed his views regarding the School's emphasis on the relevance of design outside the prevalent realm of modern design: "It's more applying design, design thinking, design methods, and things like that in fields which conventionally do not use design."[15] Exploration of these new and unexplored avenues, along with other areas of larger social relevance unattended by design intervention, can address future career concerns of the students. Since the social design education programme is in its nascent stage, the first batch of students graduated in 2016. It is only after the experience of some years of offering the programme and the performance of students as design professionals, can the outcome of its novel approach be evaluated. Nevertheless, the vision and implementation of the programme offers a tangible opportunity to re-examine and re-define contemporary design education in context of complex issues and typical challenges faced by countries like India.

Case Studies of Two Courses

Case studies of two courses offered at NID—Environmental Perception (EP) and Design Concepts and Concerns (DCC)—which were particularly referred to by experts during their interviews and stood out prominently during the analysis of the courses as well are presented below. My first-hand experience at NID—as a student of (in 1988) and, later, as a mentor for (during several modules since 1994) both these courses—corroborates the findings and adds to the depth of the case studies. My observations regarding these courses, as a jury member for the semester-end assessment for the Foundation Programme at NID as well as discussions with other mentors and students of these courses, further affirm the interpretations in both the cases.

These courses have the potential to prepare students to grasp the nuances of addressing *wicked problems* faced by the society as well as social, cultural, environmental and other issues that could arise due to their design actions. These courses typically have a significant observational and experiential component located in the 'field.' This field is a larger social setting beyond the confines of corporate set-ups that are merely seeking higher profits at any cost. Preparing a foundational understanding and larger interconnected 'any cost' implications is an important objective, or indirect outcome, of such courses. These courses also provide alternative viewpoints to students for exploring, resolving and constructing their understanding of professional design education and praxis in the context of their own individual self, image and imagination.

Both of these courses—EP and DCC—have a long history of evolution and changes. Many other design education programmes have drawn upon these courses, and the methods employed to teach them to develop their own courses that are similar in spirit or intent. Another reason for this commonality is that many teachers, who have mentored such courses at one institution, are also involved in mentoring similar courses at other institutions. To take the example of Design Concepts and Concerns, which was earlier known as Design Process, basically aims to introduce students to the method, or the process, of designing. This input is an essential part of any design education programme. However, the details, approach and the ethos of the particular course module of a specific period taught by a mentor or a group of mentors tend to vary significantly when taught by another mentor or group. As a result, the role of the individual and his or her personal belief system is further highlighted. The broad outcome may be similar, but the finer details that impact the learning and the takeaway values of students can vary considerably. This is one of the critical aspects that emerged from the case studies of DCC as well as EP.

Case Study 2: Environmental Perception

For the students newly enrolled at the design school and at an impressionable age,[16] the Foundation Programme provides formative opportunities to lay the foundation of values of future design professionals. The publication *50 Years of the National Institute of Design 1961–2011*, included an article written by Chatterjee in 1975 on the Professional Education Programme for graduate studies at NID. He wrote: "The crux of the Foundation Programme is its environmental orientation and bias... to start learning fundamentals of design more suited to the Indian day-to-day life situations."[17]

In 1976, Mohan Bhandari first experimented with a course called Environmental Exposure, with an urban focus, and its sequel called the Rural Exposure, with a rural focus. Balaram, in the teacher's comments in a course documentation of Environmental Exposure published by NID, traces the thought and social concerns behind this indigenously developed course as a part of the Foundation Programme curriculum for design students:

> At no other time in the history of humanity are we as conscious of and as concerned with our environment as we are today. Environmental issues, at the macro level, mean those related to ecology, pollution, energy, earth, sky, nature and such. For a designer involved in shaping the environment, understanding of these issues is of paramount importance. The macro level issues of the environment cannot be grasped properly unless one takes the first step of looking at the environment at the micro level – the people, places; objects and their meanings. Like all experiences, this experience of environment would also begin with sensory perception.[18]

He further says:

> A conscious observation of the environment – even if one has lived in the same environment for long – is necessary because we take our environment for granted. Drawing has been chosen as a means of closer and more detailed observation. The sketches are complimented with notes which are factual as well as reflective...
>
> The course takes place outside in the four walls of the Institute. The micro environment with its people, houses and fields is the classroom. Its time is not confined to morning, to evening working hours, but all the time. The instruction is not merely given by teacher/guides but also by the people belonging to that environment.

The Environmental Exposure course, now known as EP, has gone through several transformative phases over the years, in terms of time allocation, experimentation with the kinds of assignments and modalities of conducting the course, with the increase in the number of enrolled students, changes in coordinators of the Foundation Programme, new mentors, issues of logistics, and changing social scenarios.

Balasubramaniam, one of the foundation year students at NID in 1977 when Bhandari conducted the course, recollected that they took up a place in Ahmedabad and studied that place, a mini environment that would lead to understanding the relationships of the various forces within the ecosystem and their effects so that the systems thinking comes into play. One may not do anything with this knowledge. But the fact that students understood how society works is knowledge that would help them understand the complexities as they will have to deal with complexities during their design practice.[19]

During Bhandari's time, the course included study of an urban and a rural location. This focus subsequently shifted to study of a rural or semi-urban location. When the total number of students for the Foundation Programme at NID was within the 25–30 range, the entire batch went to a single location. In subsequent years, the enrolment of students in each batch was gradually increased. Then, the batch had to be divided in groups of around 25 students and allocated to different locations with a separate set of mentors, for better logistics. Actual time in the field also varied from one week to three weeks in a given year.

The Foundation Manual 2015–2016 of the BDes Foundation Programme at NID shows an allocation of three weeks to EP course and it is the only course listed under the category of Research and Field Work (RW). The actual time in the field is about ten days. The 'relevance' and 'objectives' of EP course as described in the manual are:

> **Relevance:** It helps to sensitize students to study the social, cultural and physical environment in which his/her design has to operate, so that it has a meaning or relevance to the people.
>
> **Objectives:**
> - To broaden one's perception about the Indian environment in terms of interrelationships and interdependence of its physical components.
> - To develop the ability to approach and mix with the people in the environment to share experiences and learn directly as they happen in life.
> - To learn to collect, analyze and represent macro to micro level information in the form of an illustrated document.[20]

The basic working methodology of the EP course involves:

- Drawing: as a tool for documenting, seeing and sharing (photography is strongly discouraged).
- Writing: as a personal journal, and annotation of drawings.
- Doing: by participating, interacting, experiencing and sharing.

Swasti Singh Ghai, currently co-coordinator of the Foundation Programme, comments on this methodology that:

> The activity of drawing makes students comfortable with local people and vice versa. Drawing enhances perception, generates curiosity, and helps

> students in slow, elaborate study of forms as components in a system. Students note down their insights along with the illustrations as records of their experiences, thus rendering the entire course into a visual essay.[21]

The basic spirit and broad objectives of EP have largely remained the same: empowering students to not merely see, but to perceive the macro and the micro, and their interrelationship, in a designerly way. Say, a local issue, or a small object in a hut (the micro) relates to the country or the world at large (the macro). Thus, this course facilitates a unique immersive experiential learning opportunity—through observation, participation, documentation and development of understanding of a given environment and its people—in the context of social, cultural, economic, developmental and political issues. Since the field of study is usually located in a semi-urban or rural setting, the batch of students and the group of mentors go off-campus and live on location for a particular duration during the course. New and 'unknown' locations arouse alertness and inquisitiveness of the students, instead of a passive acceptance of the surrounding. Different locations are chosen each year through a preliminary survey of shortlisted locations based on local receptivity, learning opportunities, and logistics.

Participation in the local activities is an aspect of the course that encourages learning by doing. It is this experiential and empirical learning that led to better perception which, in turn, facilitated clearer understanding of the milieu. The immersion of students in the local environment around planned assignments helped them navigate through the time and space provided by the course in a meaningful way. Visual and written documentation call for insightful observations that have to be accountably externalised for sharing.

The students and faculty members get together for a group discussion every evening. These discussions provide space for dialogue on social, cultural, religious, economic, political issues, incidents, problems, feelings and emotions. These are a means of catharsis for the group as they share observations, learning, eye-openers, and other varied experiences. Such discussions are significant and invaluable in a group learning process. Students process the learning against the background of their own past experiences and draw parallels with their own life experiences, away from the location of the EP course, while connections to design can continue to manifest over a long period of time.

The EP course provides an intensely immersive experience not only for students and mentors, but also for people from the host location who get involved during the study. However, this intensity is more pronounced for students who are largely from urban locations and are use to a certain kind of lifestyle. The off-campus location of the course, outside the comfort zone of the students, elevates the intensity and impact of the experience.

Korjan mentions that there was a group of students who were very upset with certain aspects of the course. These students thought that they were being overly voyeuristic and that they should not be indulging in such voyeurism. She stated that: "We were able to process that and look at the issue, whether it was really voyeuristic. And, if it was voyeuristic, then perhaps there was something wrong in the attitude with which one went there."[22] Korjan adds that they were all city students and obviously came from a certain kind of upbringing. The students felt so because they wouldn't like anyone looking at their lives in that manner. But they did relate to the fact that people in the village welcomed them, so long as they were not being voyeuristic. Korjan supports the view that there should be a lot more of such debates so that the students can process what they are uncomfortable with and decipher for themselves why they are doing, what they are doing.

Ghai, who has been associated with the Foundation Programme at NID for almost a decade, reports that

> the students, when they conclude the foundation work and in the last meeting when we ask them for feedback, most of them say that EP was the most transformative course. It continues to be the most transformative course as it was for us.[23]

Ghai was a student of the EP course at NID in 1994, for which I was one of the mentors. Ghai recalls:

> From my times, I would say total immersion in the context makes a big difference. And certainly, EP is a course, which really allows you to develop your abilities of empathy. It's not something that a faculty tells consciously, or a student also aspires consciously. I think it just happens by virtue of immersion in the context. And empathy is one of the key qualities a designer needs to have.[24]

Ghai further illustrates her views by citing examples of students who have later gone back to their EP course location to take forward ideas and issues that they came across, which required design intervention. A Film and Video student went back to Hingolgadh, to do a design project with the people there to highlight an issue they had come across during the EP course three years earlier. Another Product Design student went back to her EP course location in Anand to design implements for the farmers there.

However, for several other students, the EP experience was merely an 'outing and fun.' Another observation that needs to be noted here is the role of mentors in facilitating the quality and intensity of experience in courses like EP. This distinction came up in my own observations regarding the course as a semester-end-assessment jury member for the Foundation Programme. Due to the increase in enrolments of students in the Foundation Programme, the batches now need to be divided into four to five groups led by different groups of mentors for reasons of logistics at the place of study. Students under a particular team of mentors have displayed distinctly different levels of insight and learning, compared with those of students under another team of mentors. Mentors with a high level of interest in, and personal commitment to, social responsibility, ecological sustainability and other inter-related issues have been able to guide and sensitise their students to a much higher level of understanding. Ghai, through her extended involvement and experience with Foundation Programme at NID, corroborated these views during her interview.

Korjan, during her interview, while responding to the question about whether courses like EP have a role in sensitising students to social responsibility aspects, emphasises that it definitely does. She goes on to explain that it is "a very forward-looking and a very brave course to have been conceived." According to her, the significance of the course lies beyond merely taking the students to a rural setting. It is more in the opportunity they get to see the microcosm of a society in one village that is almost like actually seeing the whole. What one might not be able to perceive while being 'inside' a society, one can kind of see during the course as an outsider and begin to understand the relationships and dynamics at play. Having gone through this course, as a student in 1976, Korjan views that the course has not evolved as much as it should have by now. Maybe, this can be achieved by introducing other tools, beyond drawing, for the study. Maybe, there is a need to involve faculty from other disciplines, like anthropology and sociology, who could bring other dimensions and deeper engagements. These could make the EP course intellectually much more enriching and challenging.[25]

Without an integrated approach for responsible design within the curriculum, it is ultimately left to the individual students and interest of faculty members and mentors of other courses to carry forward the learning from courses like EP. A course like Design Concepts and Concerns (DCC), discussed next, significantly draws upon experiences and insights from EP to further enrich the learning of the students to foster responsible design values.

Case Study 3: Design Concepts and Concerns

Design Concepts and Concerns is essentially a course that deals with design theory and design thinking. Tracing the historical evolution of this course reveals the change in the underlying focus in its evolutionary process.[26] The course that started as 'Design Methods' in 1966 with a classical scientific focus for the post-graduate programme was, later, adapted for the graduate programme (PEP) in 1971. H. Kumar Vyas and Balaram were the key faculty members involved. As the teachers of this course started looking at processes within design, the course was re-christened 'Design Process' in 1976. The environmental focus, brought into the whole Foundation Programme by Bhandari also gave an environmental focus to Design Process course. Bhandari led the restructuring and Balaram and Ranjan developed it further.

Subsequently, in 1988, it was re-structured as DCC with a wider focus on user, the environment and systems. It was first adapted in the graduate programme and, by the early 1990s, it was adapted across all the post-graduate programmes.[27]

Sangita Shroff recalls that "in the classical design process which was taken by Kumar and other teachers in the earlier period, there was a lot of stress on understanding the user and the basic need."[28] She points out that Bhandari took the course to a different level, stressing that there was a great deal of interpretation, reinterpretation and a systemic thinking about how a device is going to impact the larger system—physical, social, political and economic. Such a holistic view got embedded in that Design Process course. Shroff recalls the time when she had taught the course for five years with Ranjan:

> in the earlier days, design process was quite a lot about the industrial design way of looking at things. You did attribute analysis; you did a user analysis; you did an environment product analysis. But it had not really come into the realm of the concepts and concerns.[29]

Students used to identify a problem that they saw, perceived and found relevant, from their surrounding environment, and do an individual project. And, in doing so, they would go through the design process to gain a better understanding beyond just theory. "We changed the name from design process to design concepts and concerns in the fifth year, when I was teaching it. And the focus became more conceptual."[30] Instead of doing individual projects, the students did group projects in the DCC course on a specific theme each year, like water, education, or economics. Then, the student groups had to find, or perceive, design opportunities within that realm.

DCC continued for over two decades, led by Ranjan along with several faculty members, who joined him in conducting this three- to five-week course, over the years, for the graduate and the post-graduate programme. Six of these faculty members were interviewed for this research to get a better understanding of the course. The process of refining and fine-tuning the course to meet the broader vision and changing scenarios was a conscious and continuous process overseen by Ranjan. He outlines the spirit of DCC course as follows:

> Design Concepts and Concerns is about Finding, Knowing, Doing and Feeling, the last word of the quartet being the most important, in my opinion. This is why the name of my course was changed from Design Methodology, that was used in the 1960s to suggest that design was a scientific discipline, and later called Design Process to suggest that it was steeped in good management; but now we understand that it is neither Science nor Management and it certainly is not Art.[31]

The DCC course aims to prepare students to see design as an "avenue for creating the unknowable, a future that is sustainable and equitable, through the bold visualisation of scenarios informed by empathy and exploration in group processes that can be shared and realized collectively, thereby closing the loop."[32] Ranjan points out: "No one is comfortable when we talk about ourselves as designers in India and the role that we should, could, or would play as a designer in the Indian context." Concurring with the *wicked problem* theory, Ranjan explained that we are often overwhelmed by the vastness and complexity of the world, feeling uncertain of where to start or how to make a difference. We may focus on opportunities that align with our skills and interests, which often lie in the comfortable and privileged end of the economy where only a small percentage of the population lives. We may try to ignore our guilt when asked about our contribution to the other 98% or the middle 60% of the population. However, students in the DCC class know that design involves looking at the needs of others, understanding their perspective, and taking action to address those needs, even if it is uncomfortable. This class emphasises a value-oriented approach to design, with the idea that the designer should act with thoughtfulness, skill, and empathy towards the user. In this model, the designer is represented as a tetrahedron, with the three base vertices representing finding, knowing, and doing, while the apex represents feeling, which is seen as the most important aspect.[33]

This course facilitates explorations in the realm of design into contemporary themes using local issues in new forms of education. Through such new forms of learning "this course provides the teachers and the students with the opportunity to deal with contextually relevant subjects in real time and a window into the future from the perspective of the school of design." Group assignments provide team spirit and diversity within a group such that

> the clarity that emerges through the experience of modelling and visualisation in these group processes provides an insight into the power of design and helps build conviction into using these processes to address the complex problems that we face in our real world.[34]

In Ranjan's opinion, "the power of design lies in visualising the future, the unknowable, through the process of open-ended context-driven investigations in design education situations." Pedagogically, in the DCC course, design is perceived "as a process of informed synthesis through the articulation of models, diagrams and scenario visualisation that could match the complexity of the real-world situations becomes the premise for the assignment design." Furthermore, 'learning by doing' and 'learning through teamwork' are two major strategies that the DCC course uses. This pedagogy led to the evolution of a group-assignment-based approach with strategically interspersed lectures, which was notably different from the project-based approach during its earlier version as a Design Process course.

A typical sequence of assignments in the DCC course can be enlisted as follows.

Assignment 1: Self-disclosure.

> Reflection about the self and looking back into one's life activities and experiences to find and locate one's preferences and belief systems including likes and dislikes and ones taboos and epistemic roots when confronted with reflexive situations in the process of design.[35]

This is a short assignment of half a day, at the end of which each student is expected to 'draw a map of themselves' on paper along with key-words and images to 'disclose themselves' to the class. The individual presentation sheets are retained on the soft-boards of the classroom for a few weeks, where the students keep coming back to it for introspection and discussion. This self-disclosure journey also turns out to be a 'self-discovery' journey in many cases; both are foundational to responsible design action.

Assignment 2: Understanding the known. Group Plumbing and Modelling:

> A selected subject or theme is given to the group which is expected to be investigated by the group of six to eight students in the form of a brainstorming session leading to the articulation of what the group knows about that particular subject or theme.[36]

It is observed that the students themselves are surprised at the extent of their 'collective knowledge.' "This is a form of mapping the known and discovering the contours of the unknown with reference to the particular batch of students."[37] This group assignment is presented in the form of a visual model built upon an appropriately selected metaphor. Such an exercise contributes to the student's understanding of this kind of search as 'a way of life for design' and 'continuous self-learning' as a way forward.

Assignment 3: Understanding business processes. In Ranjan's view, building and delivering business models are now an integral part of our understanding of design in India. This assignment is structured to give design students an understanding of business processes. In this assignment, groups of students study the working of local street food vendors. Through observations and interviews with several such service providers, the students attempt to grasp their business processes. The students visually represent the 'business model' based on their observations and findings, regarding cash flows and business strategies adopted by these micro-enterprises of these vendors. These visual models and flow charts are then presented to the rest of the class. "The presentations are used by the teachers to instruct and inform the students of the relevance of such studies and the possibility of scaling up this study to medium and large businesses in principle."[38]

To give an example, the 2010 foundation batch of 90 students was divided into six groups and studied six categories of fast-food vendors on the streets of Ahmedabad: fruit and juice vendors (juice *walla*), tea vendors (*chai walla*), *pani puri* vendors (*pani puri walla*), *pav bhaji* vendors (*pav bhaji walla*), omelette vendors (*omelette walla*) and the fried *bhajiya* vendors (*bhajiya walla*). These became the "subjects of their study of micro-enterprises which have all the business processes and strategies of a multi-national, albeit at a much smaller scale, and at much more comprehensible scale of operation."[39]

Assignment 4: Understanding the context. This assignment takes the understanding of the 'group plumbing' task forward to investigate the known and the unknown. Groups of students are encouraged to go off campus, meet experts and consultants, visit libraries and even identify unexpected locations/ people for information and to obtain expert insights based on their 'information strategy group meeting.' "This has a number of iterative sessions through which the students develop a rich set of resource persons and a much better understanding of the subject that they had set out to study in the first place."[40] This information is layered with direct observations from the field. The information gathered is shared with the class at a formal presentation mapped out in the form of a structured representation couched in a chosen metaphor that would make the image map instantly memorable and contextually relevant. These presentations are further supplemented with digital photographs and video recordings from the field. Ranjan points out: "The understanding of the subject is usually very deep and the groups usually exhibit an ability to identify numerous design opportunities that are latent in the situations studied by the group."[41] This ability to comprehend latent design opportunities within a given situation prepares students for unconventional design action.

Assignment 5: Learning to visualise scenarios. "Usually, this comprises an individual assignment dealing with exposure of the group or batch of students to a known place, event or activity location which is sufficiently rich in detail." The students use a known technique or treatment to capture the observations and draw the whole experience as a 'scenario' or a 'single story-telling image.' "This assignment in visualising the known can be later used to help students to find similar expressions in articulating the unknown, which is the design of the future object, place or event as the case may be."[42]

Assignment 6: Applying scenario visualisation to the unknown. Ranjan (2005) emphasises: "Design is indeed about visualising the future and the future is profoundly unknowable… However, design is also about shaping the future and in the shaping we change the world in small or big ways, in useful or disastrous ways."[43] This becomes the main assignment that draws upon the learning from the earlier assignments. This is a group assignment, and all the groups work on a common broad theme decided for a particular year. The carefully selected themes provide conceptual opportunities for students to address issues of the scale and nature of *wicked problems*. The assignment and its time-frame call for intensive and immersive working while articulating and expressing the known; collective brainstorming; identifying the unknown; collecting information; and gaining a deeper understanding of the subject at hand. The conceptual processes are not confined to isolated individual solutions or products. On the contrary, the students are encouraged and guided to see the larger interconnections to identify integrated design opportunities and solutions that can come together to address the issues and *wicked problems* within the given theme at strategic levels.

To give an example of this assignment, the six groups of the 2010 foundation batch were given the theme of designing six new design schools for six regions of India: the north, south, east, west, centre and northeast regions. The students explained their concepts of the proposed design schools for the specific regions through models, metaphors, mind maps and detailed articulations about the different aspects of new design education programmes. The entire exercise included vivid details of each institution's aims and objectives; mission and vision; philosophical underpinnings and policies; curriculum and pedagogical outlines; evaluation systems; faculty and student profiles; academic and administrative structures; regional location/s; infrastructure and resource requirements; finances and fund sources; public/stakeholder participation processes; collaborations and networking; social, cultural and economic impact on the local region, the country and the world. All of the six groups presented their concepts and concerns in creating the future in design education as a 'Concept Mela.' This presentation of concepts in a fair-like format (image in Figure 6.1) was open to policy-makers, administrators, stakeholders, media and the public at large over two days.

Figure 6.1 DCC 2010 Concept Mela. Groups of students with their models and metaphors to explain their concepts for the six proposed design schools for the chosen regions of India.[44]

According to Ranjan: "Design at this level has the ingredients to create the avalanche effect, a great positive mobilisation, an overwhelming quantity of something hopefully new and beneficial, with a very small designerly effort."[45]

The experiences of the DCC course shared by students from the 2010 foundation batch, further illustrate the impact of the course. One of the students points out: "DCC made me realise that we often underestimate our potential to think and think big. It has given me the confidence to think, speak and discuss even the seemingly most complex of issues."[46] This view, shared by several other students, emphasises the contribution of a course like DCC in preparing students to deal with system-level complexity and the interconnected nature of issues, necessary to deal with *wicked problems* at different levels that call for design action. Another student (from Northeast India), who was also a part of the group working on the design school for the Northeast region, reports: "The DCC course has been very enriching for me. I am originally from the Northeast region of India. But this course taught me and made me realise that the richness and potential of Northeast."[47] A careful selection of theme for each year and its contextualisation of design to the Indian situation, contributes to the possibilities of appropriate contextualisation of future work. Another student states: "DCC has been a wonderful experience for me. It has helped me to perceive things, as simple as a cup of *chai*, in a whole new manner."[48] A process of understanding the link between the micro and the macro, and empathetic understanding of the field, which might have got initiated during the EP course, gets further fortified through courses like DCC.

Comparing the overall experience from 1988 to 2010–2011, I remember that, earlier, students gained an understanding of the design process with application on a small scale, which was focused on a physical end product or its prototype, more like a typical client assignment. Whereas over the two decades of my involvement, the structure and the scope of the assignments, the content of the lectures and discussions during the DCC course got oriented towards the larger impacts of design action, demands of the assignments made it an immersive experience. While developing the individual capacity of the students, the DCC course is able to emphasis the collaborative spirit to handle complexities of today's world and virtually deal with issues or project of any scale. The social, cultural, economic, political and ethical issues are so integrated in the course that the students get a lens to see the larger worldview to locate their own concepts, ideas, intentions and solutions in a much broader context, while dealing with several issues related to the environment, society, governance, producers, and consumers.

Korjan, one of the team members of the DCC course for over a decade, describes that, at the core, the course holds the view of looking at everything holistically and systemically. Therefore, even these young students are thrown into addressing complex issues and big challenges so that they can see the interconnections. At the end of the course, the students emerge feeling optimistic and empowered, even though they are not creating concrete and tangible results. They definitely have a sense and confidence that they can address something complex; they can make an attempt to understand it and make definite contributions within it. In today's world there is an increasing need to address complexities and to look at systems.[49]

However, Korjan reports that, in the past couple of years, the 'dumbing down' of the DCC course has happened at NID, where one is just looking at 'silly little toaster problems.' She clarifies that sometimes one may need certain exercises like that too, but it also speaks of the kind of future that designers are being envisioned for. Korjan goes on to question:

> Are you creating someone who can actually look at very complex things and handle that complexity? Or are you looking at someone who can just take simple problems and solve them, and not look at any difficult problems as such?

She also doubts the kind of designers the industry really wants. This connects back to Balasubramaniam's description of 'Photoshop donkeys.' Korjan is of the opinion that the strong thinking which was present behind the DCC course and its development is missing in the new version, again renamed as Design Process. She, along with other mentors, has taught two editions of this new course but finds a lack of coherent thinking behind it, and the students are back to doing small individual projects. Korjan mentions that she, in fact, tried to find out why they were trying to change it, but couldn't find any consistent thinking behind the change.[50]

In Korjan's opinion, it is possible to change this; but there has to be clarity about the 'why.' She said:

> the only feedback I got was from colleagues and from the disciplines that the students opted for was that students were not prepared enough and that they needed a different kind of input in the first year. And, I didn't think that was valid because a lot of that input has to come in that discipline itself.

In her view, the kind of attitude that developed in the students was quite valuable. She argues that even if we were to change a course, it needed to be critically evaluated and must 'apply ourselves to our own processes.' The course achievements and missing inputs could be mapped by talking to some of the students who took the course as well as some of the faculty members who taught the course. Through a designerly process, it could be determined what was working and what was not. And, at the end of the process, it would be easier to arrive at the aspects that need to be added or changed.

> None of the people who were teaching the new course had taught DCC, except me. So, for all of them, this was a new course altogether, without

any reference to what we had done before. So, it was very difficult to even dialogue about what we are achieving here, and what we were achieving before.[51]

Analysis of the Three Case Studies

The case study of the Ambedkar University's School of Design illustrates that when the vision and mission of a design education programme, along with a larger social mandate, is integrated into its curriculum, courses and pedagogic framework, it leads to a high probability of socially responsible outcomes. This ensured the coming together of the kind of faculty members and students who are aligned with the institutional mandate. This integration is demonstrated through the case study of AUD's design education programme.

Comparatively, in other contemporary design education programmes in which there is a gap between the social mandate and its integration in curricula, courses and pedagogic frameworks, institutional thrusts on social responsibility values cannot be ascertained. In the absence of substantial institutional emphasis on these values, the presence of a few courses like EP and DCC become highly significant. However, in situations where there is lack of institutional focus on socially responsible design values, the explorations and outcomes of even these potential courses become highly dependent on the interest, inclination and intention of individuals—faculty members as well as students.

The unique immersive and experiential course format of EP provides an opportunity to closely understand a small town or village. This has the possibility of laying the foundation for an empathetic understanding of social, cultural, economic and political scenarios of certain sections of diverse India. Many students report to have carried away everlasting and insightful impressions from these experiences, which they continue to draw upon for years to come.

The highlight of the DCC course is the development of student's ability to deal with complexity, scale and the interconnected nature of *wicked problems* and understandings of collaborative working. Such abilities are critical in addressing issues of social responsibility in future design thinking and action.

Findings from the case studies concur with the views of the experts interviewed for this research. Most of the experts were of the opinion that discussions related to ethics, values, beliefs and orientation of designers in the context of social responsibility, environmental concerns, governance and related *wicked problems* are avoided or limited to individual interests of concerned faculty members and students. The exceptions were institutions like AUD's School of Design, where these values were integrated in the entire programme. Otherwise, the few specific courses, which had the scope and opportunities to bring forth, contemplate, question and discuss these issues and foster related values, become highly dependent on individuals. Thus, there were no assured and consistent programme inputs in these seemingly personal, yet critical, areas of design education.

The experts strongly highlighted the lack of definite academic guidelines or curricular emphasis on issues of social responsibility as an integral part of the contemporary design education programmes in India. This became evident during the case study of both EP and DCC where these courses were modified and changed for administrative convenience or other nebulous reasons without appropriate academic considerations.

Any course like DCC can be effective due to its empowering spirit of revealing the process of going about designing, problem-solving, finding solutions, and processes of converting a thought into deliberate design action. However, dealing with the intent and sensitive judgement behind the thought process of deliberate action is a complex area to incorporate within the pedagogy. The spirit reinforced by the mentors through queries and issues raised during the course and the inclination of the students to address responsible design issues play a significant role in the development of these values. The mentors can play a significant role in addressing issues and dilemmas faced by students regarding values, ethics, personal beliefs, and life's missions and goals in the context of being a design professional at a very personal level.

Bryan Lawson, psychologist, architect and design researcher, in his book *How Designers Think: The Design Process Demystified*, explains the significance of the individual designer's personal beliefs in context of design thinking:

> the designer does not approach each design problem afresh with a *tabula rasa*, or blank mind, as is implied by a considerable amount of the literature on design methods. Rather, designers have their own motivations, reasons for wanting to design, sets of beliefs, values and attitudes.[52]

which serve as "guiding principles" of a designer's thought and action. A designer's personal beliefs—orientation and understanding of justice, equity, economics, class, caste, colour, gender, religion, and politics—influences and reflects the creation process of a small piece of communication or a large system. The evolution of these beliefs and values during the education and training of the designers also influences the priority of choice in what they set out to address and resolve. Both the students as well as the faculty members need to determine and strengthen the 'guiding principles' to build strong character for a socially responsible practice irrespective of the arena of design practice.

Notes

1 Findeli, A. Rethinking Design Education for the 21st Century: Theoretical, Methodological, and Ethical Discussion. *Design Issues*, 17.1 (2001): pp.5–17. https://www.jstor.org/stable/1511905.
2 Fry, T. *Becoming Human by Design*. London and New York: Berg, 2012.
3 Lodaya, A., personal communication, 16 September 2016.

4 Bharat Ratna Dr B.R. Ambedkar Vishwavidyalaya, Delhi is officially also known as Ambedkar University, Delhi or AUD.
5 Dr Bhimrao Ramji Ambedkar (1891–1956).
6 AUD Website - About Us - Vision and Mission', n.d.
7 AUD Website-Academics-Schools-School of Design. n.d.
8 Balasubrahmanyan, S. 2016. Op cit.
9 School of Design, 2016.
10 Bhatt, J. Op cit.
11 Ibid.
12 Ibid.
13 Balasubrahmanyan, S. 2016. Op cit.
14 Bhatt, J. Op cit.
15 Md. Farooqui, S., personal communication, 18 July 2016.
16 Students in the age group on 17–19 years, after completing general schooling, join the graduate studies.
17 The Professional Education Programme (PEP) for graduate studies at NID was started in 1970.
18 Balram, S., & Patel, N. N. *Adlaj Village -Environmental Exposure: A Corse Documentation.* Ahmedabad: NID, 1992. pp.6–7.
19 Balasubramaniam, A. Op cit.
20 Foundation Manual: B. Des. Foundation Programme. NID 2015–2016.
21 National Institute of Design. *50 Years of the National Institute of Design 1961–2011.* Ahmedabad: NID, 2013.
22 Korjan, R. Op cit.
23 Ghai, S. S., personal communication, 22 July 2016.
24 Ibid.
25 Korjan, R. Op cit.
26 The historical evolution has been traced on the basis of a slide titled "Design Methods to Design Concepts & Concerns" shown as a part of a presentation by M. P. Ranjan at a seminar at NID in August 1995.
27 Ranjan, M. P. Design Concepts and Concerns: The Avalanche Effect from NID 2012. Retrieved from http://design-for-india.blogspot.in/2012/07/evolution of dcc-course-at-nid.html.
28 Shroff, S., personal communication, 22 July 2016.
29 Ibid.
30 Ibid.
31 Ranjan, M. P. The Avalanche Effect: Institutional Framework and Design as a Development Resource in India, privately published, 2002. p.7.
32 Ranjan, M. P. Creating the Unknowable: Designing the Future in Education. Presented at the Sixth International Conference of the European Academy of Design, Bremen: University of the Arts, 2005. p.12.
33 Ranjan, M. P. The Avalanche Effect: Institutional Frameworks and Design as a Development Resource in India, privately published, 2002. pp.1–14.
34 Ranjan, M. P. 2005. Op cit.
35 Ibid., p.8.
36 Ibid., pp.8–9.
37 Ibid., p.9.
38 Ibid., p.9.
39 Ranjan, M. P. Business Models for Designers 2010: Learning from the Field. 2010. Retrieved from http://design-concepts-and-concerns.bogspot.com/2010/04/conceptmela-awareness-coclusion-for.html.
40 Ibid.
41 Ranjan, M. 2005. Op cit. p.9.
42 Ibid.

43 Ibid., p.10.
44 Ranjan, M. P. Concept Mela. Awesome Conclusion for DCC 2010. Retrieved from http://design-concepts-and-concerns.blogspot.com/2010/04/concept-mela-awesome-conclusion-for.html
45 Ibid.
46 Personal communication, March 26, 2010.
47 Ibid.
48 Ibid.
49 Korjan, R. Op cit.
50 Ibid.
51 Ibid.
52 Lawson, B. *How Designers Think: The Design Process Demystified* (4th ed.). Oxford and Burlington, MA: Elsevier/Architectural, 2006.

7 Changing the Change

Design Education for Social Responsibility

The orientation of contemporary design education towards preparing designers for client service and demands of the industry or the market is well established in the previous chapter. Designing to fulfil the needs of consumers, or designing new needs—real or psychological—and attempting to fulfil them as products, services, visuals and modification of perception/behaviour dominates design education programmes today. Thus, it contributes to promoting a consumerist world by design. Not by training designers to design, but by specifically training designers to fulfil the 'designs' of the 'production nexus' that can only thrive on growing consumerism.

However, it is clear beyond doubt that an infinite greed-oriented consumerist world is unsustainable within the finite resources on this Spaceship Earth. René Spitz, chairman of the IFG advisory board and author of the book *HfG IUP IFG Ulm 1968–2008*, on the history of the Ulm School of Design, expresses his concerns in an interview to *Dezeen*[1] magazine in 2012: Social responsibility has fallen down the agenda of today's designers and design schools. "[It] is more important than ever. In recent years this has been forgotten… We have failed to formulate new answers to the question of what societal responsibility is today—specifically, beyond phrases and slogans."[2] The example of classroom discussion on the values of social responsibility, quoted earlier, supports this claim. Furthermore, it demonstrates the keenness of students to apply socially relevant values and ethics in their design practice. However, this mood has still to become a part of the mainstream institutional thought process, mandate and support. "We have already lost a substantial time. If we are looking for the human face of globalization, then design schools will have to make the choice quickly!"[3] The call for action on multiple design fronts is sharper with a sense of urgency.

The earlier reference to design anthropologist Tunstall's lecture and presentation at IICD, about her work with aboriginals in contemporary Australia, can be recalled here. Parallels can be drawn with Native Americans, African tribes, Dravidians, Aryans, Caucasians and others, and human legacy of

DOI: 10.4324/9781003383352-8

power play, greed, robbing, looting, genocide, intrusion, wars, invasions, forced conversions, slavery, oppression, discrimination, injustice, inequity and marginalisation or wiping out the diversity of cultures, beliefs, values, knowledge, aesthetics and creative expressions. We can see the continuation of these ideas even today: in the outline of the third world, the second and the first world; in the appalling divide of the rich and the poor; biases attached to skin colours, sexual orientations, religious beliefs and practices, clothing and appearances; the Eastern and the Western divide or the North and the South block. The list can go on. However, this is not to say that there has been no positive exchange. The point here is how design students can be sensitised and equipped to take their own stand and contextually deal with wider issues of the real world as they design. Design education programmes need to accept the relevance of incorporating such significant and sensitive issues as a part of the curricula with the agenda of social responsibility. A wider and deeper understanding about such issues can assist in understanding the political undercurrents of people, cultures, environments and economics of society as a whole. This would also prepare designers to use propositional politics as a tool to bring about socially responsible change.

There are courses in some design education programmes which attempt to deal with such issues in varying depths and intensities. In addition to the three case studies discussed in the previous chapter, there were some courses offered earlier at NID where such immersive opportunities were available. One example was for Industrial Design students at NID, through the Craft Documentation course, where students took up detailed documentation of a selected traditional craft at the location of the craftsperson. Such a course provided several intensive opportunities to interact at the socio, economic and cultural level, besides documenting the craft processes. They inform as well as sensitise the individual student.

The Science and Liberal Arts (SLA) programme at NID provides a variety of theoretical inputs related to aesthetics, narratives, theatre, semiotics, cultural studies, etc., for better meaning-making and context-building for design. The scope of the SLA programme needs to be explored and expanded to realise its hidden potential. Some of the courses at NID provide opportunities that cross over and dissolve rigid boundaries. This is becoming increasingly essential for a holistic approach through design. However, such rigidness is a common feature of a typical design programme. Buchanan also describes the need to overcome such 'rigid boundaries' through his description of the new liberal art of design thinking. He says:

> It points toward the impossibility of relying on any one of the sciences (natural, social, or humanistic) adequate solutions to what are the inherently wicked problems of design thinking. Finally, it points toward something that is often forgotten, that what many people call 'impossible' may actually only be a limitation of imagination that can be overcome by better

> design thinking. This is not thinking directed toward a technological 'quick fix' in hardware but toward new integrations of signs, things, actions, and environments that address the concrete needs and values of human beings in diverse circumstances.[4]

Multi-dimensional, issue-based immersive courses can be successful in sowing seeds of responsible design amongst students. Design education programmes need to focus on the nurturing of these seeds. Without this, the seeds may lie dormant for long periods of time. A close examination of the NID courses discussed as case studies reveals that only a few students start making connections beyond these specific courses and carry it forward for wider applications. And there are many other students who see these courses in isolation, merely as a requirement to be completed.

The ethical orientation of the individual student, mentor and even the design school becomes the guide to responsible design action. With reference to the direct and indirect contribution of design to several issues that surround us on this Spaceship Earth, the concern for ethical considerations and dilemmas associated with them is natural for many and cannot remain avoidable for others, involved with a design education programme and design praxis. The three classical orders of ethical considerations introduced earlier with reference to the personal belief system can be applied in the context of design too. These considerations can be examined both at the epistemological context of a design education programme and the metaphysical aspect of the individual—design educator, design student or design professional—in the context of social responsibility. Findeli says: "There can be no responsible design without a responsible designer, i.e., education should be directed to the development of an individualistic ethics." He explains that unless ethics in design education is not considered in particular, "any general discussion about ethics, morals, ethical theory, deontic/utilitarian ethics, etc., becomes almost meaningless."[5] Well-known authors of the book titled *Good Work: When Excellence and Ethics Meet,* outline five levers for Good Work: "Creating new institutions, expanding the functions of existing institutions, reconfiguring the membership of existing institutions, reaffirming the values of existing institutions and taking personal stands."[6] They explain,

> We speak not just of 'good work' but of 'good work in difficult times.' Not difficult necessarily in terms of daily creature comforts but in terms of people's ability to know the right thing to do and remain in their professions.

It is useful to distinguish two lines of development: competence and character in the context of the development of an individual designer, which essentially points out the overemphasis on competence and the plight of ethical, moral and spiritual values in the contemporary world. Papanek's view about the spiritual value as design intent argues: "It is the intent of the designer as well as the intended use of a designed object that can yield spiritual value." He further explains, "The performance of such services to our fellow humans and the planet will help inwardly. It will nourish our soul and help it to grow. That's where spiritual values enter design."[7]

In describing the order of design, Ranjan identified three broad levels:

> The first level of design recognises material form and structure;
> The second level is influenced by the impact and effect in terms of function and feeling; and the
> The third level is the order of design for value—meaning and purpose.

This level is shaped by the higher values in our society and by the philosophy, ethics and spirit that we bring to our products, events, systems and services. Ranjan located spirituality as the high point in this third order (refer to Figure 7.1).

Victor Margolin argues that

> a meta-narrative of spirituality can empower designers and technologists to better understand design as a form of action that contributes to social wellbeing. It can link design to a process of social improvement that becomes the material counterpart of spiritual evolution.[8]

Thus, a spiritual source can be used as a *g.o.d* for almost any kind of design process. Such a source provides us with insights, ideas and guidance and, as a

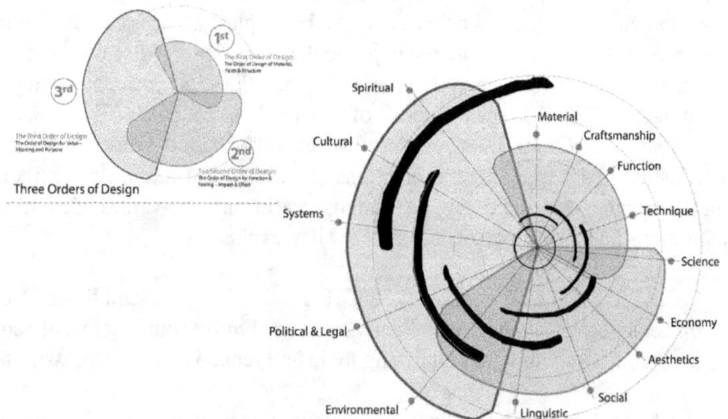

Figure 7.1 "Three Orders of Design" by M. P. Ranjan presented as Keynote Address, "Hand-Head-Heart: Ethics in Design" at 4th National Design Conference at Istanbul Technical University, Istanbul.

soothing consequence and peace of mind. A spiritual approach is used to see things in a different way that enables us to interpret reality in a more true or ideal way.

The significance of ethics, spirituality and other components of the personal belief system in the context of design action have been discussed in earlier chapters. The views of Findeli, Papanek, Ranjan, Margolin, Nelson, Stolterman and other design educators and designers have also advocated and established the significance of ethics and spirituality in the act of creation through design. Even so, these are not seen as a part of the mainstream thought process or approach in design education and praxis. I found sparse and implicit references to ethics, spirituality and other components of the personal belief system discussed earlier, and I identify the need to be explicit in the context of responsible design education now. My research established the significance of the designer's personal belief system as a whole (along with ethics and spirituality) and the need to be included as a significant part of a responsible design education programme,[9] in searching and exploring answers to unanswered questions, unrecognised needs and unresolved dilemmas in the context of design and the future of this planet.

Future Action

Future action in the context of design education needs to be both at the institutional and at the individual level. Here individuals would include both individual students and individual faculty members.

Howard Gardner, in his work titled *Changing Minds*, sheds light on the inceptive stages of an individual's achievement of good work, which involves two orders of mind change:

> First, it requires a belief that Good Work is an important part of life, a phenomenon too vital to be left to chance or to others… Second, it requires the creation of experiences that are likely to increase the incidence of Good Work.[10]

This has to be well recognised and established within a design education programme—to inspire and prepare students for the first and encourage, facilitate, integrate, showcase and promote the second one from within the programme.

Similarly, to bring about change towards social responsibility in a design education programme, three inceptive stages are proposed which need to be further elaborated for actualisation:

1 Recognition of need
2 Articulation of commitment
3 Models of implementation

Recognition of Need: This book has outlined the significance and need for socially responsible design beyond doubt. However, for any positive action in this direction, design schools have to recognise this as the basic fabric of their education programme in totality. As seen in earlier examples, it cannot be a one-off, negotiable part of the programme. In addition, it has to be recognised as the basic ethos by each and every faculty member and staff of the programme. Only then will the students recognise and understand the significance of social responsibility. Furthermore, the recognised need has to be externalised as clearly articulated understanding and commitment for change.

Articulation of Commitment: The articulation of a responsible design commitment and action plan, through publicly shared documents, such as an institutional manifesto, vision document, and mission statement, can be a crucial move towards its implementation in a design school. A clearly articulated mandate places the responsible design agenda on a common shared platform beyond the personal commitment of teachers, and individual students. Through such documents, the design programme—as a department, or as an independent design school/university—shares its philosophy, intent and action outline. The publicly declared commitment and open accessibility of documents create self-imposed moral and ethical thrust to keep up with the declarations.

This common shared understanding, amongst the faculty and others within the programme, facilitates translation to the next logical steps of incorporating it into the academic syllabi, course abstract papers and practical incorporation into the courses.

Prospective students, as well as existing students, see this for their better understanding. Other design schools, the industry and the public at large can see it too. It can not only have a ripple effect but also increase the chances of better implementation due to self-imposed public pressure, till the time such a spirit starts becoming a normative part of design education programmes.

The institutional commitment needs to form the basis of the commitment of individual faculty members to operate on behalf of the institution. A minimum standard or a pre-decided set of commitments might well form a part of their service contract itself. Moreover, the individual faculty members should be encouraged to further detail their undertaking to raise their individual commitment level even higher above the minimum standard. Such resulting personal manifestos should also be publicly articulated and shared. Furthermore, there should be full scope and practice of incremental improvements in these personal manifestos, based on further practical experiences, new understandings and refined thought processes.

Each design student should also be introduced to a basic set of responsible design commitments. As their engagement becomes more serious with design philosophy and action, like their faculty members, students should also be required to articulate their individual manifestos and continue a process to further refine their commitments. Personal design manifesto formulations should be a formal part of the design education system. Each academic year, students should have the option to choose a mentor to guide their manifesto articulation process. The availability of a mentor, along with access to other professionals like psychologists and peer group discussions, could assist in addressing personal and professional dilemmas around the manifesto building process.

The vital component in the practical implementation of intent and commitment is the individual's micro-interpretation of details of purpose. Through the term micro-interpretation, attention is invited to the finer details that need to be implemented to make a real difference, compared to the largely accepted macro-interpretations. Such macro-interpretations tend to be basic and limited in scope, and can easily overlook critical details to implement responsible design action in the real sense and of a higher order.

Similarly, institutional commitment to responsible design education in their manifestos, guidelines or vision documents should also offer scope for reinterpretations and periodic upgradability to reconcile with new experiences from pedagogy and praxis as well as changing socio-cultural and environmental challenges. However, a thorough articulation of intent is not enough; implementable action plans must be outlined for actualisation and materialisation of intent or purpose.

Models of Implementation: With reference to the earlier discussion on the personal belief system, it is clear that

> the designer does not approach each design problem afresh with a *tabula rasa*, or blank mind, as is implied by a considerable amount of the literature on design methods. Rather, designers have their own motivations, reasons for wanting to design, sets of beliefs, values and attitudes.

However, for some designers, this collection of attitudes, beliefs and values are confused and ill-formed, for others they are more clearly structured. Bryan Lawson expounds, "whether they represent a collection of disjointed ideas, a coherent philosophy or even a complete theory of design, these ideas can be seen as a set of 'guiding principles' of a designer's thought and action."[11] These 'guiding principles' of both the students as well as the faculty members need to be strengthened to build strong character that can stand by their articulated commitments to responsible design.

But strong character is difficult to achieve, particularly at a time when religious, communal, and family traditions and values are weak and uncertain, and the principle messages conveyed by the mass media are irrelevant at best. Accordingly, many people look to schools—private and public, elementary, and secondary, undergraduate and graduate, as forgers of character.[12]

The design education programmes also have to share a social responsibility in forging the character of their students into responsible creator-designers as well as responsible citizens. But to achieve this task, first and foremost, design schools will need educators who are proficient, well-trained, sensitive and responsible. Then, and only then, will they have the moral ground to teach what they practice and succeed in guiding transformation amongst students.

Training of Trainers: Paulo Freire, renowned Brazilian educationist, refers to Marx in emphasising the critical need for the educator's education: "The materialist doctrine that men are products of circumstances and upbringing, and that, therefore, changed men are products of other circumstances and changed upbringing, forgets that it is men that change circumstances and that the educator himself needs educating."[13] To keep pace with or even to remain relevant in this rapidly changing world, the design educators, more than ever before, need to have sustained access to relevant learning modules. The very nature of design education necessitates dealing with extremely varied issues and problems, which have to be reciprocated with similarly diverse opportunities of theoretical and practical learning opportunities for the mentors.

> If we speak of integrated design, of design-as-a-whole, of unity, we need designers [as well as design educators] able to deal with design process comprehensively… Their education would need to be less specialized and include many disciplines now considered to be only distantly related to design, if related at all.[14]

To lead a programme in responsible design, educators need to prepare themselves beyond conventional methods of teaching in a design education programme. First and foremost, they have to be prepared to implement the responsibility mandate of the institution and, furthermore, their individual manifestos described earlier. In doing so, they have to equip themselves with theories, issues, current trends and a deeper understanding of society, culture, environment, people, economy, polity, equity, ethics, sustainability, prosperity and other real-world issues. Design educators also need to acknowledge the role of an individual's personal beliefs, responsibility, values, and spirituality, to lead a holistic responsible design education programme. Faculty members need to have a clear understanding of irresponsible design and awareness of prevalent unethical practices in the design profession as well. With all these in their background, a design educator can fulfil the critical role of mentoring future creator-designers.

Hence, design educators will have to re-examine, modify or even change many of their older ways of teaching, guiding, approving, and even assessing student projects and assignments.

Responsible Design Filter: To ensure consistent design input and faithful implementation of a responsible design programme for a reliable outcome, calls for a significant shift in ways of teaching and learning for responsible design action. I have proposed the idea of a 'filter system' for the design process of socially responsible design. Broadly, these filters are to provide ways of identifying and segregating design propositions, ideas, and decisions that could contribute to irresponsibility from those that ensure responsible design decisions.

This filter system would have an array of filters. There could be basic sets that could be used as default. The whole filter system would be open to permutation, combination and modification of the basic filter sets, as well as the creation of new ones, to arrive at an appropriate order. Filters could also be customised to vary their filtering strength to deal with specific instances or particular projects. For instance, there could be a set of filters deemed suitable for first-year design students. As the students advance in their learning and understanding, they may be given another version of these filters with more stringent parameters. Progressively, they could be prepared to deal with more complex real-world situations.

To gain further insight, let us look into a few examples:

'Responsibility filter' could be constructed by incorporating various components of responsibility expected of a design professional. The earlier discussion on 'Redefining Social Responsibility of Designer as Creator' is used as a basis to elucidate the example of the responsibility filter. The design propositions for a particular project have to pass through each of the following filter points, to be acceptable for further action:

- Responsibility to the Client
- Responsibility to the Consumer
- Responsibility to Governance
- Responsibility to Society
- Responsibility to the Environment
- Responsibility to Self.

If a design decision fails to pass through, then it would either need to be reconsidered for modification or be discarded. Otherwise, the filter component itself would have to be readjusted for its level of strength or consciously altered with justification.

Similarly, the 'ethics filter' will have components such as environmental ethics, social ethics, business ethics and so on. There could be a separate personal ethics filter that could be applied by the individual during the design decision-making process, over and above the general ethics filter. A 'personal ethics filter' would be necessary to implement a personal manifesto. There could be several such filters with varied construction components and their intensities. Finally, when all the design decisions successfully 'pass' through the array of filters, the resulting design outcome would well presumably pass the 'litmus tests' for social responsibility. Figure 7.2 presents the idea of the 'filter system' discussed above, as a schematic diagram.

A responsible design education programme has to incorporate these filters in its *modus operandi.* All of the course structures, individual assignments, and specifically independent projects that students take up in their senior

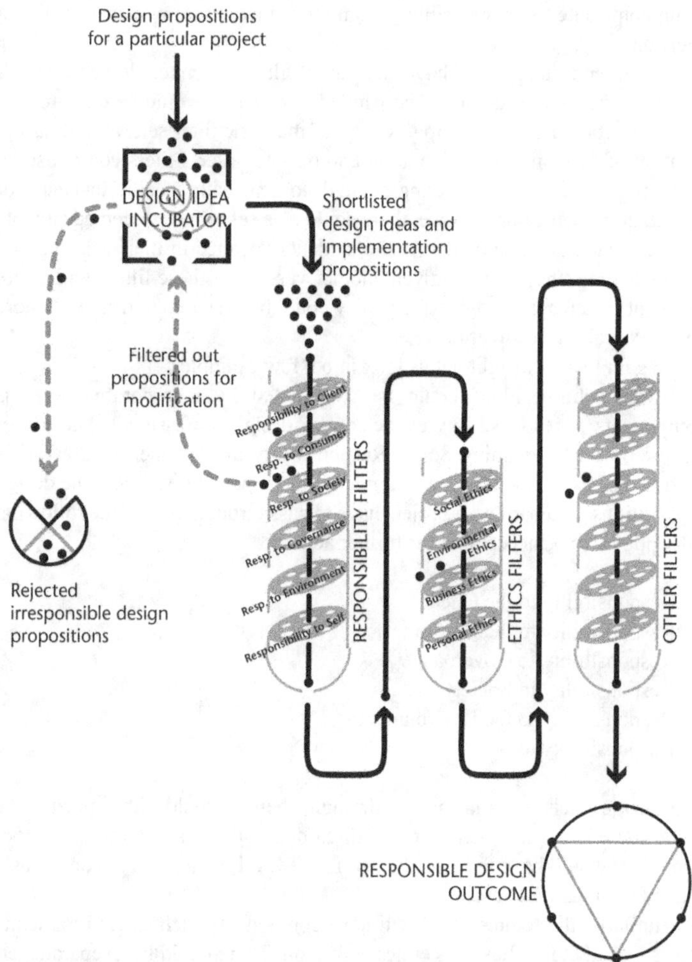

Figure 7.2 Visual representation of a 'Filter System' for implementation of socially responsible design.

years, to apply and demonstrate their learning, would need to pass through appropriate filter systems. This would also ensure that courses, which incorporate the values of responsible design, are not one-off, isolated or elective courses. To establish an end-to-end filter system, the assessment rubric will need to meticulously incorporate the filter system. Types of filters used, their strength parameters, process of filter construction and resulting quality of design decisions have to pass the responsibility litmus test of the assessment process as well as the articulated personal manifesto.

These filter systems can be applied to professional design practice equally well. The versatility of such filter systems provides ample scope for development and pursuit of excellence. Independently or as collectives/networks—design schools, professional bodies and individuals can figure out ways of examining, identifying and integrating new approaches to filtering out irresponsible design from education programmes and praxis. With the ever-growing influence and significance of professional design in everyday life, and with growing concerns over its environmental and socio-cultural consequences, now seems to be that critical time, maybe a tipping point, to bring about a paradigm shift in our ways of teaching, learning and practising design.

Notes

1 Dezeen magazine is an influential architecture and design blog on the Internet. Retrieved from http://www.dezeen.com.
2 Chalcraft, E. Designers and Social Responsibility: New Book on Ulm School of Design. *Dezeen*, 26 November 2012.
3 Athvankar, U. A. Globalization and the New Mantra of Design Education for India. In V. S. Katiyar & S. Mehta (Eds.) *Design Education Tradition and Modernity: Scholastic Papers from the International Conference* 2005 (pp.493–506). Ed Ahmedabad National Institute of Design 2007.
4 Buchanan, R. Wicked Problems in Design Thinking. *Design Issues*, 8.2 (1992): pp.5–21.
5 Findeli, A. Op cit. p.13.
6 Gardner, H., Csikszentmihalyi, M., & Damon, W. *Good Work: Where Excellence and Ethics Meet*. New York: Basic Books, 2001.
7 Papanek, V. Toward the Spiritual in Design. In R. Roth & S. K. Roth (Eds.) *Beauty Is Nowhere: Ethical Issues in Art and Design* (pp.37–48). Amsterdam: G+B Arts International.
8 Victor, M. Design, the Future and the Human Spirit. *Design Issues*, 23.3: pp.4–15. https://doi.org/10.1162/desi.2007.23.3.4.
9 Nelson, H. G., & Stolterman, E. Op cit. p.248.
10 Referred to in the book *Good Work: When Excellence and Ethics Meet* by Howard Gardner, Mihaly Csikszentmihalyi, and William Damon, 2001.
11 Lawson, B. *How Designers Think: The Design Process Demystified* (4th ed.). Oxford: Burlington, 2006.
12 Gardner, H., Csikszentmihalyi, M., & Damon, W. Op cit. p.246.
13 Freire, P. *Pedagogy of the Oppressed*. Trans. Myra Bergman Ramos. London: Penguin Books, 1996.
14 Papanek, V. *Design for the Real World: Human Ecology and Social Change* (2nd rev.). London: Thames and Hudson, 1985. p.295.

Conclusion

The omnipresence of design is the indispensable reality of human civilisation. The highly networked pluralistic post-industrial world will be no exception; in fact, designerly ways will probably be the way of life and survival, more so in the future than ever before. Contemporary problems of environment and society are rooted to a large extent in greed and manipulation exemplified by the 'consumerist world by design'—an anthropocentric act of world creation. A designer, in the act of creating a consumerist world, assumes the antithetical roles of a facilitator and manipulator,[1] instead of being a creator-designer who would guarantee inclusive and appropriate design action for harmonious coexistence and abundance for all, beyond mere sustainability. I have argued here that greedy manipulation is manifesting in the long-term unsustainability of humans and their socio-cultural diversities, and the delicately balanced and highly interdependent ecosystem of the Spaceship Earth. Social responsibility has to be seen as a broad expression denoting a complex inclusive network and not limited to human society in isolated exclusivity.

Therefore, there is a pronounced need for designers who would not only understand the possibilities of their role as creator-designers but also assume the responsibilities of their design action, to provide design solutions for an equitably viable future.

Where can such designers come from? Design education has a crucial role to play in fulfilling this responsibility, by nurturing the development of students, the future designers, who are socially responsible, ethically rich and spiritually balanced.

Some of the main arguments of this book are mentioned below. These seek to explain the inadequate output of such responsible design professionals from mainstream design schools:

1 The Occidental spirit of development and industrialisation and schools like Bauhaus and Ulm has had definitive influence on modern design education across the world. However, the 'imported influence' depended on what was perceived to be appropriate at that time. Developing and newly independent countries like India perceived design as a contributor to the

DOI: 10.4324/9781003383352-9

process of implementing models of development based on modern science, technology and industrialisation.

2 The modern design education programmes are primarily geared to provide employable trained human resource to serve the trending demands of industry to profitably feed created needs of the consumerist world. Developing the professional competence of students has been the focus of such programmes and inculcation of social responsibility and ethical values have not been distinctly prioritised.
3 The courses on responsibility issues are rare and they end up appearing in isolation. Only a few students who wish to explore alternate ways of professional practice see them as useful. Social responsibility is yet not recognised as one of the foundational objectives of design schools.
4 Due to the lack of broad institutional support, the onus of carrying the responsibility agenda comes on to individual faculty member's interests and commitments, which may vary and fluctuate. A consistent input or even a bare minimum input across classes of students cannot be ensured.
5 The preparedness and inclination of individual students to deal with issues of social responsibility vary considerably. Only some students display eagerness and sensitivity to integrate these issues in their thinking and working. Interests in such issues, most often, have linkages to the individual's past experiences and beliefs from before joining a design school, and to some strong revelations during the course of design study.

To address these issues, offering isolated courses or mere tweaking of existing courses and curriculum does not appear to be enough. Design schools have to overcome their outlook of being service-providers to the industry by merely producing skilled design professionals. They have to assume the role of 'conscience keepers' of the profession. For this, design education programmes have to be in sync with key individuals—the design educator, the design student and the trained professional designer—and recognise the pivotal role of these individuals, which have been outlined in this book.

There is a recognition here of the responsibility to the individual in the list of responsibilities of a designer. It is seen as all-encompassing, basic and as the most consequential unit, at the root of every social action. Only if an individual's sense of responsibility towards oneself is fully developed, can the individual reflect oneself in responsible action at large. My central argument is seen in the context of design education, as the compelling need to focus on the development of the individual design educator and design student, the future design professional. By acknowledging the individual as the seed of change, this book underlines in bold, the need for strengthening character, along with training for competence amongst individual design students and re-orientation of design educators. The development of unique individual character in harmony with the interests of humankind and others, can pave the path for responsible design action.

An integrated development of competence and character needs to be seen as an important personal strength of an individual. However, individualistic values of character and competence may not be enough. I could not agree more with Gardner et al., who point to a further direction that appears pertinent to design education.

> Optimal development of a person involves fulfilling two potentials that we all have: *differentiation* and *integration.* A differentiated person is competent, has character, and has achieved a fully autonomous individuality. This is the highest goal of Western cultures. An integrated person is someone whose goals, values, thoughts, and actions are in harmony; someone who belongs to a network of relationships; someone who accepts a place within the system of mutual responsibilities and shared meanings. In many Eastern cultures, it is integration that is held to be the highest goal of human development. A future worth striving for, in our opinion, is one where a person can develop both differentiation and integration to their fullest extent.[2]

For the 'optimal development' of individuals to contribute to responsible designers—both as differentiated and integrated—the design education programme needs to address issues beyond the Oriental and Occidental divide, to prepare future 'glocal' designers, with global understanding and local sensitivity, for the pluralistic world society spread across contemporary networks.

Further, this book ventures to place the metaphysical aspects of design at the core of the transformation required by design education programmes for responsible design. These programmes should recognise non-materialistic, non-dualistic and non-absolutistic worldviews and realities, and recognise the role of the personal belief system, with components like ethics, secularity and spirituality, as foundational to fostering values of social responsibility amongst designers. In addition, this would elevate awareness about 'others' and reinforce tolerance, understanding and compassionate sensitivity through design in the face of increasing fundamentalism and violence. It will probably make it easier in relating and sensitively interacting with co-workers and clients from diverse socio-cultural backgrounds and varied personal beliefs.

The recognition of the need for responsible design has to be followed up with a public articulation of commitments at the institutional as well as individual levels. The articulation of a responsible design commitment and action plan, through publicly shared documents such as manifestos, vision documents, and mission statements, create public pressure to perform by being available in the public domain and open to audit. Furthermore, such public commitments by institutions and individuals provide them legitimate ethical grounds for responsible design advocacy with industries and governments aimed at revising existing policies. This would help to elevate general awareness and wider acceptance of designers with the socially responsible ethos. Perhaps, this would prepare the ground for propositional politics and design activism.

This book recognises that implementing responsible design into the education programmes along with professional praxis are complex tasks. In an education programme, training of trainers can be seen as the logical point of intervention to initiate any change and sustain the process of development. Design educators need to rethink their patterns and models of imparting design education and the design schools ought to actively facilitate these processes. Further, the book proposes a 'filter system' to sieve out irresponsible design. The filter system could be incorporated as a part of mainstream courses, develop new specifically immersive courses and integrate in central discussions at the core of the programmes, courses, assignments, projects, assessment processes and in the philosophical underpinning of responsible design action both at the level of the education programme and professional practice.

Certainly, the complexities are much more than what is presented in the simplified depiction of the filter system here and require future research and work. Interviews and empirical data collected from more students, cross-section of faculty members, administrators of several design schools and practising design professionals could better inform future research in this area. Identification and analysis of more courses and their outcome could provide deeper insights for future work.

Earlier in this book, designers were identified in two broad categories: Designers and Responsible Designers. However, in the light of extensive discussion, the book identifies an apparent need to reframe the nomenclature proposed earlier. In the given social and environmental conditions, it is not a matter of choice, but a matter of urgency for designers to act with responsibility. Responsible action has to be a fundamental approach and cannot be seen as an additional 'extra' quality. Though there could be several levels of grey in categorising the different kinds of designers, it is now proposed that the nomenclature should be starkly re-organised as: Designers and Irresponsible Designers.

Unaccountable irresponsible action is always easier and convenient without having to go against the flow or face confrontational situations by following commitments to higher standards of values, ethics, social and environmental responsibilities. Here, it is worth pointing out that, it may not necessarily be the designer or the design school that does not recognise the problem. But not understanding or not seeing the root of the problem is 'convenient' or 'politically correct.' Possibly, the design fees or the security of salary depends on not recognising the real problem or not questioning the consequences of myopic design action.

Under the re-categorisation, it will be evidently tougher to qualify as a designer, in comparison to qualifying as an irresponsible designer. Fostering the values of a 'designer,' a creator-designer in the real sense, calls for a paradigm shift in the current approach to education and practice of design. Responsible design action in the larger socio-cultural and environmental context requires efforts and advocacy that transcends commercial or political gains.

Notes

1 Portraying the designer as a manipulator and the idea of manipulation via design could be seen as uncomplimentary, since it is largely perceived as a negative term. However, manipulation of material, process, behaviour and idea can be done for positive outcome or with unscrupulous intentions. In fact, it is the intent behind the action that becomes the guiding spirit of manipulation.

2 Gardner, H., Csikszentmihalyi, M., & Damon, W. Op cit. p. 243.

Annex A

Survey Questionnaire

This questionnaire is a part of an on-going research on design education in India.

The aim of this research is to examine the role of design education in India in imparting values of socially responsible design to their students, the future design professionals.

The purpose of this questionnaire is to gain insights about issues related to the research area from respondents associated with design education programmes in India. Their current or past associations could be as design educators or design students or those design students who subsequently became design educators. The involvement of design educators could have been full-time, part-time/adjunct/visiting faculty member.

There is no specific right answer to a question. The questions are aimed at gaining from each respondent's views and understanding, based on their own past experiences and impressions regarding design education in India.

1. How have you been involved with design education in India?* *(Select one option)*	
As current or past design educator (full-time faculty member or part-time visiting faculty member)	O
As current or past design student	O
Both (as design student in the past and subsequently as design educator—current or past, full-time or part-time)	O
Not involved with design education in India	O

It should take about 25–30 minutes of your time to respond to this survey. As a respondent you are requested to answer all the questions in the given sequence. At the end of the questionnaire, you will have the option of choosing whether or not would you want to give permission of allowing your real name to be referred to in the research document.

If you have any query or concern regarding the questionnaire or the research, do not hesitate to contact the researcher Sanjeev Bothra by emailing to sanjeevbothra@gmail.com or calling on +91–141–4022838.

* Required Information

Branching Instructions: IF ANSWER TO [QUESTION# 1 is (Not involved with design education in India)] THEN STOP, and say: 'YOU HAVE FINISHED THIS SURVEY'. Otherwise go to QUESTION#2

2. According to you, has design contributed to the growth of consumerism and related industrial expansion in India? *(Select one option)*	
Major contribution	O
Minor contribution	O
No contribution	O
Not sure	O

3. Do you see a growth or drop in demand for design professionals in India? *(Select one option)*	
Significant growth	O
Slow growth	O
Slow drop	O
Significant drop	O
Not sure	O

4. According to you, in the Indian context, is there a rise or fall of interest in professional design education among students aspiring to pursue professional studies? *(Select one option)*	
Significant rise	O
Slow rise	O
Slow fall	O
Significant fall	O
Not sure	O

5. Do you see an increase or decline in the number of design education programmes/institutions in India? *(Select one option)*	
Significant increase	O
Slow increase	O
Slow decline	O
Significant decline	O
Not sure	O

6. Are you aware of an increase or decrease in the number of seats per batch of students at design education programmes in India? *(Select one option)*	
Significant increase	O
Slow increase	O
Slow decrease	O
Significant decrease	O
Not aware	O

7. Do you see a rise or reduction in the course fees of design education programmes in India? *(Select one option)*	
Significant rise	O
Slow rise	O
Slow reduction	O
Significant reduction	O
Not aware	O

8. In your view, generally how successful are the design education programmes in India in preparing their students for the job market/industrial demand? *(Select one option)*	
High success level	O
Medium success level	O
Low success level	O
Not successful	O
Not sure	O

9. According to you, what is the main focus of design education programmes in India? *(Select one option)*	
To be a profit-making educational activity for the institution	O
Prepare designers to meet the demands of job market/industry	O
Prepare designers to address larger issues related to the society and environment through design	O
Not sure	O

10. Can design interventions also have unintended outcome beyond what is primarily intended by the designers? *(Select one option)*	
Yes	O
No	O
Not sure	O

11. Could there be undesired impacts on the society at large, beyond efficacy for the intended end-user of design? *(Select one option)*	
Yes	O
No	O
Not sure	O

12. Can imparting of socially responsible design values by design education programmes influence the larger social impact of design outcome of their students? *(Select one option)*	
Yes	O
No	O
Not sure	O

13. How do you view the need for imparting values of socially responsible design through design education programmes in India? *(Select one option)*	
Critical and foundational	O
Somewhat significant	O
Not necessary	O
Not sure	O

14. In your experience, do the design education programmes in India impart values of socially responsible design? *(Select one option)*	
Yes	O
No	O
To some extent	O
Not sure	O

15. Do you see a conflict between the need to impart values of socially responsible design and to prepare students as per commercial job market expectations? *(Select one option)*	
Yes	O
No	O
To some extent	O
Not sure	O

16. According to you, which are the top five design education programmes/ institutions in India?
[Please list in descending order—top most ranked programme at (1.) and so on…]

(a) 1.
(b) 2.
(c) 3.
(d) 4.
(e) 5.

17. Have you come across documents, publicly shared (on websites or otherwise), by design education programmes/institutions in India, articulating their mandate/ vision/mission referring to values of socially responsible design? *(Select one option)*	
Yes	O
No	O

18. On a scale of 0 to 10, how would you rate the commitment of design education programmes in India towards imparting values for socially responsible design? *(0 being not committed, 10 being highly committed)*

0	O
1	O
2	O
3	O
4	O
5	O
6	O
7	O
8	O
9	O
10	O

19. In your view, what is the most significant factor in imparting socially responsible design values among design students? *(Select one option)*

The institutional mandate/vision/mission oriented towards values of socially responsible design	O
The syllabus and course components directed towards values of socially responsible design	O
The inclination of individual design educators towards values of socially responsible design	O
None of the above	O

20. What could place a stronger thrust in imparting socially responsible design values within design education programmes in India? *(Select one option)*

Appropriate restructuring of syllabus and courses	O
Training and orientation of design educators	O
Both the above	O
None of the above	O

21. In your experience, are the design educators in India adequately prepared in their understanding of socially responsible design values? *(Select one option)*

Most of them are adequately prepared	O
Some of them are adequately prepared	O
Most of them are not adequately prepared	O
Not sure	O

22. Whether there is need or no need for 'training of trainers' programmes for design educators to better prepare them in understanding values of socially responsible design and imparting these values? *(Select one option)*

There is a great need	O
There is some need	O
There is no need	O
Not sure	O

23. What is the key influencing factor in fostering values of socially responsible design in design education programmes in India? *(Select one option)*

Influenced by institutional mission/vision and the syllabus	O
Influenced by attitude/values of individual teachers/faculty members	O
Influenced by personal belief formulated by past experiences and upbringing of students	O
Influenced by the demands of the job market	O
None of the above	O

24. Can the application of socially responsible design values in design practice contribute to a more sustainable future? *(Select one option)*

Yes	O
No	O
Not sure	O

25. In your view, is it possible to integrate the values of socially responsible design as an integral part of a design practice? *(Select one option)*

Yes	O
No	O
Not sure	O

26. Do you see a market demand for socially responsible design among future employers? *(Select one option)*

Yes	O
No	O
Not sure	O

Follow the branching rules in the sequence given below. Jump to the Question as specified in the branching rule if all the conditions specified in the rule are satisfied. Rule 1: IF ANSWER TO {Question# 1 is [As current or past design educator (full-time faculty member or part-time visiting faculty member)]} THEN GO TO Question# 35

ABOUT YOUR INSTITUTION/PROGRAMME (as a Design Student)

27. Name the design education institution/programme in India where you last studied or are currently enrolled at:

(a) Name:
(b) Year of enrolment:

28. Are you aware whether the programme has a mission/vision document or an institutional manifesto? *(Select one option)*

Yes	O
No	O
Don't know	O

29. In your experience as a design student, what percentage of courses focuses on imparting skills to meet the demands of the industry/the job market? *(Select one option)*

10%	O
20%	O
30%	O
40%	O
50%	O
60%	O
70%	O
80%	O
90%	O
100%	O

30. In your experience as a design student, what percentage of your courses focuses on imparting values of socially responsible design? *(Select one option)*

10%	O
20%	O
30%	O
40%	O
50%	O
60%	O
70%	O
80%	O
90%	O
100%	O

31. Can you name some of the courses you had undergone that potentially imparted values of socially responsible design?

32. As a student, did you undertake any project/s that had strong component of socially responsible design? If yes, please share descriptive title of such project/s and year in which the project was done.

33. If applicable, name the other Indian design education institutions/programmes you have been involved with as a student in the past:

34. Please indicate the total number of years of your engagement as a formal design student:

(a)

Follow the branching rules in the sequence given below. Jump to the Question as specified in the branching rule if all the conditions specified in the rule are satisfied. Rule 1: IF ANSWER TO {Question# 1 is [Both (as design student in the past and subsequently as design educator—current or past, full-time or part-time)]} THEN GO TO Question# 35 Rule 2: IF ANSWER TO {Question# 1 is NOT [As current or past design educator (full-time faculty member or part-time visiting faculty member)]} THEN GO TO Question# 44.

ABOUT YOUR INSTITUTION/PROGRAMME (as a Design Educator)

35. As a design educator, how have you been involved with design education in India? *(Select one option)*

Full-time faculty member	O
Part-time faculty member (including visiting faculty member or adjunct faculty member)	O
Both the above (as full-time as well as part-time faculty member over the years)	O
Other (please specify)	O

36. Total number of years of your involvement (full-time/part-time) with design education in India:

37. Name the Indian design education institution/programme that you are currently associated with or were last associated with as a (fulltime/part-time) design educator:

(a) Name:

38. Are you aware whether that programme has a mission/vision document or an institutional manifesto? *(Select one option)*

Yes	O
No	O
Don't know	O

39. In your experience as a design educator, what percentage of courses focuses on imparting skills to meet the demands of the industry/the job market? *(Select one option)*

10%	O
20%	O
30%	O
40%	O
50%	O
60%	O
70%	O
80%	O
90%	O
100%	O

40. In your experience as a design educator, what percentage of your courses focuses on imparting values of socially responsible design? *(Select one option)*

10%	O
20%	O
30%	O
40%	O
50%	O
60%	O
70%	O
80%	O
90%	O
100%	O

41. Can you name some of the courses in your programme that potentially imparted values of socially responsible design?

42. Have any of your students done project/s that had a strong component of socially responsible design? *(Select one option)*

None of them	O
A few of them	O
Many of them	O

43. If applicable, name the other Indian design education institutions/programmes you have been involved with as a design educator (full-time/part-time) in the past:

44. Demographic information—About you

(a) First Name: (b) Last Name:
(c) Email Address:

45. Would you consent for your name being quoted in the research report?

YES	O
NO	O

46. If required, would you be willing to be further contacted for an interview to share your detailed insights regarding the research area?

YES	O
NO	O

47. Age: How old are you?

Under 21 years	O
Between 21 and 25 years	O
Between 26 and 30 years	O
Between 31 and 35 years	O
Between 36 and 40 years	O
Between 41 and 45 years	O
Between 46 and 50 years	O
Between 51 and 55 years	O
Between 56 and 60 years	O
Between 61 and 65 years	O
Between 66 and 70 years	O
71 or more years	O

48. Gender:

Male	O
Female	O

49. Highest academic qualification:

Bachelor degree or equivalent	O
Master degree or equivalent	O
Ph.D.	O
Other (Please specify)	O

50. Please specify the name of the institution of your highest academic qualification:

51. Please specify your area of specialisation:

52. Have you been involved with professional design practice? *(Select one option)*

No	O
Yes (please specify number of years)	O

Annex B

List of Respondent Affiliations (Current or Past)

Design education programmes/institutions/departments represented.

1	Aayojan School of Architecture, Jaipur
2	Acharya School of Design, Bangalore
3	Ahmedabad School of Fashion Technology, Ahmedabad
4	Ahmedabad University, Ahmedabad
5	Apeejay Institute of Design, Jalandhar
6	Arch Academy of Design, Jaipur
7	Banasthali Institute of Design (BID), Faculty of Design, Banasthali Vidyapith
8	Bhanwar Rathore Design Studio, Ahmedabad
9	Buddha Institute of Architecture, Udaipur
10	Centre for Environmental Planning and Technology, Ahmedabad
11	CEPT University, Ahmedabad
12	Chamarajendra Academy of Visual Arts (CAVA), Mysore
13	College of Fine Arts, Trivandrum
14	Craft Development Institute (CDI), Srinagar
15	Dayalbagh Educational Institute, Agra
16	Department of Design, Nirma University, Ahmedabad
17	Department of Design, State University of Performing And Visual Arts (SUPVA), Rohtak
18	Design & Innovation Academy, Noida
19	Design and Innovation Lab, IIITD, Delhi
20	Design Development Academy (DDA), Gandhinagar
21	Dhirubhai Ambani Institute of Information and Communication Technology (DAIICT), Gandhinagar
22	DJ Academy of Design, Coimbatore
23	Faculty of Architecture & Ekistics, Jamia Millia Islamia, New Delhi
24	Faculty of Fine Arts, University of Rajasthan, Jaipur
25	FLAME University, Pune
26	Footwear Design & Development Institute (FDDI), Noida
27	GD Goenka School of Fashion & Design (SOFD), GD Goenka University, Gurgaon
28	GLS Institute of Design, Ahmedabad
29	Goa College of Architecture, Panaji
30	Goa College of Art, Panaji
31	Guwahati School of Architecture & Design, Guwahati
32	ICAT Design & Media College, Chennai
33	Indian Institute of Art & Design, New Delhi

34	Indian Institute of Crafts and Design (IICD), Jaipur
35	Indian Institute of Technology (IIT)
36	Indian Institute of Technology (IIT), Department of Design, Delhi
37	Indian Institute of Technology (IIT), Department of Design, Guwahati
38	Indian Institute of Technology (IIT), Department of Architecture and Planning, Roorkee
39	Indian Institute of Technology (IIT), Industrial Design Centre (IDC), Mumbai
40	Indian School of Design & Innovation (ISDI), Mumbai
41	Indubhai Parekh School of Architecture (IPSA), Rajkot
42	INIFD, Jaipur
43	Institute of Fashion Technology, Navi Mumbai
44	Interior Design Program, Nagpur University
45	International Collage for Girls (ICG), Jaipur
46	Jaipur Polytechnic College, Jaipur
47	Kalaraksha, Bhuj
48	Kamla Raheja Vidyanidhi Institute for Architecture and Environmental Studies, Mumbai
49	Kerala State Institute of Design, Kollam
50	Khyati School of Design, Ahmedabad
51	Madhav Institute of Technology and Science, Gwalior
52	Maharaja Ranjitsinh Gaekwad Institute of Design, MSU, Baroda
53	Maharaja Yashwant Rao Institute of Design, Indore
54	Malaviya National Institute of Technology (MNIT), Jaipur
55	Manipal University, Jaipur
56	MICA, Ahmedabad
57	MIT Institute of Design (MITID), Pune
58	National Institute of Design (NID)
59	National Institute of Design (NID), Ahmedabad
60	National Institute of Design (NID), Bangalore
61	National Institute of Design (NID), Gandhinagar
62	National Institute of Design (NID), Kurukshetra
63	National Institute of Design (NID), Vijayawada
64	National Institute of Fashion Technology (NIFT)
65	National Institute of Fashion Technology (NIFT), Delhi
66	National Institute of Fashion Technology (NIFT), Hyderabad
67	National Institute of Fashion Technology (NIFT), Jodhpur
68	National Institute of Fashion Technology (NIFT), Kangra
69	National Institute of Fashion Technology (NIFT), Kannur
70	National Institute of Fashion Technology (NIFT), Mumbai
71	National Institute of Fashion Technology (NIFT), Patna
72	National Institute of Fashion Technology (NIFT), Raebareli
73	National Institute of Technology, Tiruchirappalli
74	Nirmala Niketan, Mumbai
75	Pearl Academy, Chennai
76	Pearl Academy, Delhi
77	Pearl Academy, Jaipur
78	Pearl Academy, Mumbai
79	Poornima University, Jaipur
80	Premlila Vithaldas Polytechnic (PVP) SNDT Women's University, Mumbai
81	Rachna Sansad Academy of Architecture, Mumbai
82	Raffles Millennium International, Ahmedabad
83	Royal School of Architecture, Royal Global University, Guwahati
84	RV College of Engineering, Bangalore

85 Satyajit Ray Film and Television Institute, Kolkata
86 Satyam Fashion Institute, Noida
87 School of Architecture & Design, Vivekananda Global University, Jaipur
88 School of Creative Art, Design and Media Studies (SCADMS), Sharda University, Delhi
89 School of Design, Ambedkar University (AUD), Delhi
90 School of Design, Doon University, Dehradun
91 School of Design, IILM University, Gurgaon
92 School of Design, Mody University of Science and Technology, Lakshmangarh
93 School of Design, NMIMS, Mumbai
94 School of Design, UPES, Dehradun
95 School of Fashion Design, Jaipur National University, Jaipur
96 School of Planning and Architecture (SPA), Delhi
97 Sir JJ College of Architecture, Mumbai
98 Sir JJ Institute of Art, Mumbai
99 Sophia College for Women, Mumbai
100 Spectrum Institute of Design, New Delhi
101 Sri Aurobindo College of Art and Communication, New Delhi
102 Srishti Institute of Art Design & Technology, Bangalore
103 State Institute for Development of Arts & Crafts (SIDAC), Bhubaneswar
104 State Institute of Design (SID), Rohtak
105 Sushant School of Design, Ansal University, Gurgaon
106 Symbiosis Institute of Design, Pune
107 The Bhawanipur Design Academy, Kolkata
108 The Design Village, Noida
109 Thinking Bucket, Jodhpur
110 TVB School Of Habitat Studies, New Delhi
111 Unitedworld Institute of Design (UID), Ahmedabad
112 Vogue Institute of Fashion Technology, Bangalore
113 Whistling Woods International, Mumbai
114 Wigan and Leigh College, Bangalore
115 Women's Polytechnic, New Delhi

Annex C

Survey Data: Representing Course Foci

Consolidated views of survey responses indicate the percentage of courses that focus on imparting skills to meet the demands of the industry/the job market and the percentage of courses that focus on imparting values of socially responsible design. This information has been utilised to find out the dominance of one type of course over other and separately represent the views of design educators and design students.

Q39. In your experience as a design educator, what percentage of courses focuses on imparting skills to meet the demands of the industry/the job market?

Response Categories	%	Percentage of total respondents
10%	1%	
20%	1%	
30%	4%	
40%	11%	
50%	19%	
60%	22%	
70%	18%	
80%	15%	
90%	5%	
100%	4%	
		20% 40% 60% 80% 100%

Q40. In your experience as a design educator, what percentage of your courses focuses on imparting values of socially responsible design?

Response Categories	%	Percentage of total respondents
10%	7%	
20%	14%	
30%	14%	
40%	17%	
50%	14%	
60%	13%	
70%	5%	
80%	9%	
90%	2%	
100%	5%	
		20% 40% 60% 80% 100%

Q29. In your experience as a design student, what percentage of courses focuses on imparting skills to meet the demands of the industry/the job market?		
Response Categories	**%**	**Percentage of total respondents**
10%	3%	
20%	5%	
30%	7%	
40%	10%	
50%	15%	
60%	19%	
70%	21%	
80%	13%	
90%	3%	
100%	3%	
		20% 40% 60% 80% 100%

Q30. In your experience as a design student, what percentage of your courses focuses on imparting values of socially responsible design?		
Response Categories	**%**	**Percentage of total respondents**
10%	6%	
20%	12%	
30%	15%	
40%	17%	
50%	15%	
60%	9%	
70%	11%	
80%	8%	
90%	3%	
100%	3%	
		20% 40% 60% 80% 100%

Annex D

Expert Interviews: Profile of Interviewees

No	*Interviewees*	*Gender*	*Studied design*	*Yrs. in design education*	*Yrs. in design profession*	*Link to design edu. progrms.*	*Interview mode*
1	Interviewee A	M	Yes	23	33	7	In-person
2	Interviewee B	M	Yes	20	24	4	In-person
3	Interviewee C	F	Yes	33	40	8	In-person
4	Interviewee D	M	Yes	27	30	15	In-person
5	Interviewee E	M	Yes	11	21	3	In-person
6	Interviewee F	F	Yes	8	9	1	In-person
7	Interviewee G	M	Yes	27	47	6	In-person
8	Interviewee H	F	Yes	13	32	8	Online
9	Interviewee I	F	Yes	8	9	2	In-person
10	Interviewee J	M	Yes	11	14	3	In-person
11	Interviewee K	M	Yes	22	27	3	In-person
12	Interviewee L	F	Yes	8	8	1	In-person
13	Interviewee M	F	Yes	23	27	4	In-person
14	Interviewee N	F	Yes	30	35	11	In-person
15	Interviewee O	M	Yes				Online
16	Interviewee P	F	Yes	35	35	12	In-person
17	Interviewee Q	M	Yes	25	29	1	In-person
18	Interviewee R	F	Yes	21	27	4	In-person
19	Interviewee S	F	Yes	12	19	4	In-person
20	Interviewee T	M	Yes	18	22	8	In-person

References

About Us | Srishti Institute of Art, Design and Technology. (n.d.). Retrieved 19 November 2018, from https://srishtimanipalinstitute.in/about-us

Academic Programs: Industrial Design Centre (IDC) IIT Bombay, India. (n.d.). Retrieved 19 November 2018, from http://www.idc.iitb.ac.in/academics/index.html.

Aims and Concerns: Industrial Design Centre (IDC) IIT Bombay, India. (n.d.). Retrieved 19 November 2018, from http://www.idc.iitb.ac.in/about/aims.html.

Balaram, S. (2005). Design Pedagogy in India: A Perspective. *Design Issues*, *21*(4), 11–22. www.jstor.org/stable/25224015.

Balasubrahmanyan, S. (2012). *Genesis of Design Education in India: The Warp and Weft of Local - Global Contexts* (Diss). Ahmedabad: CEPT University.

Bason, C. (Ed.). (2017). The Changing Nature of Design. In *Leading Public Design* (1st ed., pp.33–52). Retrieved from http://www.jstor.org/stable/j.ctt1t88xq5.7.

Best, J. W., & Kahn, J. V. (2012). *Research in Education* (13th ed.). New Delhi: PHI Learning Private Limited.

Bogner, A., Littig, B., & Menz, W. (Eds.). (2009). *Interviewing Experts* (2009 ed.). New York: Palgrave Macmillan.

Bonsiepe, G. (2006). Design and Democracy. *Design Issues*, *22*(2), 27–34.

Bonsiepe, G. (2013). The Centre/Periphery Antinomies of Design in Latin America. *Towards Global Histories of Design: Postcolonial Perspectives*. Presented at the Design History Society Annual Conference 2013, Ahmedabad.

Brown, T. (2009). *Change by Design: How Design Thinking Transforms Organizations and Inspires Innovation*. New York: HarperCollins Publishers.

Buchanan, R. (1992). Wicked Problems in Design Thinking. *Design Issues*, *8*(2), 5–21.

Carrington, D. (2016, August 29). The Anthropocene Epoch: Scientists Declare Dawn of Human-Influenced Age. *The Guardian*. Retrieved from https://www.theguardian.com/environment/2016/aug/29/declare-anthropocene-epoch-experts-urge-geological-congress-human-impact-earth.

Carson, R. (1962). *Silent Spring* (1st ed.). Boston, MA: Houghton Mifflin.

Chatterjee, A. (2005). Design in India: The Experience of Transition. *Design Issues*, *21*(4), 4–10. https://doi.org/10.1162/074793605774597514.

Chatterjee, A. (2015, October). *Design as Tool for Economic Development in India*. Presented at The First Mahesh Buch Memorial Lecture, Bhopal. Retrieved from https://nchse.org/Buchmemorial.html.

Churchman, C. W. (1967). Guest Editorial: Wicked Problems. *Management Science*, *14*(4), B141–B142.

Creswell, J. W. (2007). *Qualitative Inquiry & Research Design: Choosing among Five Approaches* (2nd ed.). Thousand Oaks, CA: Sage Publications.

Creswell, J. W. (2014). *Research Design: Qualitative, Quantitative and Mixed Methods Approaches* (4th ed.). Thousand Oaks, CA: SAGE Publications, Inc.

Cross, N. (2006). *Designerly Ways of Knowing*. London: Springer.

Davis, M. (2017). *Teaching Design: A Guide to Curriculum and Pedagogy for College Design Faculty and Teachers Who Use Design in Their Classrooms*. New York: Allworth Press.

Dawson, C. (2009). *Introduction to Research Methods* (4th ed.). Oxford: How to Content.

Design As a Global Profession of MIT Institute of Design, Pune. (n.d.). Retrieved 19 November 2018, from https://www.scirp.org/(S(lz5mqp453edsnp55rrgjct55))/reference/referencespapers.aspx?referenceid=2588186.

Design in India. (n.d.). Retrieved 29 November 2017, from Design in India website: http://www.designindia.net.

Diethelm, J. (2014). *A Paradigm Shift in Design Thinking*. Retrieved from http://www.academia.edu/7153275/A_Paradigm_Shift_in_Design_Thinking.

Dutta, A. (2007). *The Bureaucracy of Beauty: Design in the Age of Its Global Reproducibility*. New York: Routledge.

Eames, C., & Eames, R. (1991). The Eames Report April 1958. *Design Issues*, *7*(2), 63–75.

Erlhoff, M., & Marshall, T. (Eds.), Bruce, L., & Lindberg, S. (Trans.). (2008). *Design Dictionary: Perspectives on Design Terminology* (1st ed.). Basel: Birkhäuser Verlag AG.

Findeli, A. (2001). Rethinking Design Education for the 21st Century: Theoretical, Methodological, and Ethical Discussion. *Design Issues*, *17*(1), 5–17. Retrieved from https://www.jstor.org/stable/1511905.

Fisher, T. (Ed.). (2016). Reconstructing Design Education. In *Designing Our Way to a Better World* (pp. 55–63). Retrieved from http://www.jstor.org/stable/10.5749/j.ctt1c0gm71.9.

Friedman, K. (2012). Models of Design: Envisioning a Future Design Education. *Visible Language*, *46*(1/2), 132–153.

Fry, T. (2009). *Design Futuring: Sustainability, Ethics and New Practice* (English ed.). Oxford: Berg Publishers.

Fuller, R. B. (1969). *Operating Manual for Spaceship Earth*. Carbondale: Southern Ilinois University Press.

Hampson, F. O., & Reppy, J. (1996). *Earthly Goods: Environmental Change and Social Justice*. Ithaca, NY: Cornell University Press.

Heller, S., & Vienne, V. (Eds.). (2003). *Citizen Designer: Perspectives on Design Responsibility*. New York: Allworth Press.

Heskett, J. (2005). *Design: A Very Short Introduction*. Oxford: Oxford University Press.

India Design Council (Ed.). (2014). *Conference Proceedings: Designing Design Education for India – 13th March to 15th March 2013 – Pune, India*. Ahmedabad: India Design Council.

Katiyar, V. S., & Mehta, S. (Eds.). (2007). *Design Education - Tradition and Modernity: Scholistic Papers from the International Conference, DETM 05*. Ahmedabad: National Institute of Design.

Kelvin, N. (Ed.). (1999). *William Morris on Art and Socialism*. Minneola, NY: Dover Publications.

Klein, D., & Phillips, K. (2011). Sustainable Design: An Educational Imperative. *The Journal of Technology Studies*, *37*(1/2), 69–77.

Liedtka, J., Salzman, R., & Azer, D. (2017). *Design Thinking for the Greater Good: Innovation in the Social Sector*. Retrieved from http://www.jstor.org/stable/10.7312/lied17952.

Manzini, E. (2015). *Design, When Everybody Designs: An Introduction to Design for Social Innovation* (R. Coad, trans.). Cambridge: The MIT Press.

Margolin, V. (1998). Design for a Sustainable World. *Design Issues*, *14*(2), 83–92. https://doi.org/10.2307/1511853.

Mathur, I. S. (2014). *Design Education in India: Retrospection, Introspection, and Perception* (1st ed.). Ahmedabad: National Institute of Design.

Michl, J. (2010). A Case against the Modernist Regime in Design Education/by Jan Michl. Retrieved 27 June 2012, from Jan Michl (Oslo, Norway): Design Theory website: http://www.janmichl.com/eng.apartheid.html.

National Design Policy – Approved by Government of India. (2011). https://indiadesigncouncil.org/pdf/National_Design_Policy.pdf.

National Institute of Design. (2013). *50 Years of the National Institute of Design 1961–2011*. Ahmedabad: National Institute of Design.

National Institute of Design - Curriculum Objectives. (n.d.). Retrieved 19 November 2018, from https://www.nid.edu/academics/curriculum-objectives/detail.

National Institute of Design - History & Background. (2015). Retrieved 12 June 2023, from http://www.nid.edu/about/history-of-nid.

National Institute of Design – Mandate (Mission, Vision, Values). (n.d.). Retrieved 12 June 2023, from https://www.nid.edu/about/mandates.

Nehru, J. (1985). *An Autobiography*. New Delhi: Oxford University Press.

Nehru, J. (1989). *The Discovery of India* (Century ed.). Delhi: Oxford University Press.

Nelson, H. G., & Stolterman, E. (2003). *The Design Way: Intentional Change in an Unpredictable World*. Englewood Cliffs, NJ: Educational Technology Publications.

NIFT 2019 Admissions. (n.d.). National Institute of Fashion Technology, Ministry of Textiles, Government of India.

Papanek, V. (1985). *Design for the Real World: Human Ecology and Social Change* (2nd Rev.). London: Thames & Hudson.

Patel, D. (2014). *India: Contemporary Design: Fashion, Graphics, Interiors*. New Delhi: Roli Books Pvt Ltd.

Patton, M. Q. (2001). *Qualitative Research & Evaluation Methods* (3rd ed.). Thousand Oaks, CA: SAGE Publications Inc.

Pedagogy - MIT Institute of Design. (n.d.). Retrieved 12 June 2023, from https://www.mitid.edu.in/pedagogy/.

Postgraduate Professional Programs -2019–2020 | Srishti Institute of Art, Design and Technology. (n.d.). Retrieved 12 June 2023, from https://srishtimanipalinstitute.in/programs/2-year-postgraduate-program-in-arts-professional-practices.

Potter, A. (2006). Curriculum Assessment. In J. L. Green, G. Camilli, P. B. Elmore, & American Educational Research Association (Eds.), *Handbook of Complementary Methods in Education Research* (pp.141–159). Washington, DC: Lawrence Erlbaum Associates; Published for the American Educational Research Association.

Ranjan, M. P. (2002). The Avalanche Effect: Institutional Frameworks and Design as a Development Resource in India. Privately Published, pp.1–14.

Ranjan, M. P. (2005, March). *Creating the Unknowable: Designing the Future in Education.* Presented at the 6th International Conference of the European Academy of Design, Bremen.

Ranjan, M. P. (2007, June 14). Design for India: Mission Statement [Blog]. Retrieved 15 June 2017, from Design for India website: http://design-for-india.blogspot.in/2007/06/mission-statement.html.

Ranjan, M. P. "DCC 2010: Foundation Batch 2009–10." *Design Concepts & Concerns*, 30 December 2009. http://design-concepts-and-concerns.blogspot.com/2009/

Ranjan, M. P. (2013a, January 13). Design for India: Web of Connections: Indian Design Education with Influences from the HfG Ulm. Retrieved 13 January 2018, from Design for India website: http://design-for-india.blogspot.com/2013/01/recognising-roots-nid-accorded-status.html.

Ranjan, M. P. (2013b, July 2). *Design Thinking Models_Primer 2013.* Retrieved from http://academia.edu/3848991/Design_Thinking_Models_Primer_2013.

Rawson, P. S. (1988). *Design.* Englewood Cliffs, NJ: Prentice-Hall.

Rittel, H. W. J., & Webber, M. M. (1973). Dilemmas in a General Theory of Planning. *Policy Sciences*, *4*(2), 155–169. https://doi.org/10.1007/BF01405730.

Schön, D. A. (1983). *The Reflective Practitioner: How Professionals Think in Action.* New York: Basic Books.

Scotford, M. (2005) Introduction: Indian Design and Design Education. *Design Issues*, 21 (4), 1–3. http://www.mitpressjournals.org/toc/desi/21/4.

Scott, D., & Morrison, M. (2006). *Key Ideas in Educational Research* (1st ed.). London and New York: Continuum International Publishing Group.

Shulman, L. S. (2005). Signature Pedagogies in the Professions. *Daedalus*, *134*(3), 52–59. https://doi.org/10.1162/0011526054622015.

Simon, H. A. (1996). *The Sciences of the Artificial* (3rd ed.). Cambridge: MIT Press.

Sotamaa, Y. (2009). The Kyoto Design Declaration: Building a Sustainable Future. *Design Issues*, *25*(4), 51–53.

Stake, R. E. (2005). *Multiple Case Study Analysis* (1st ed.). New York: The Guilford Press.

Thackara, J. (2006). *In the Bubble: Designing in a Complex World.* Cambridge, MA: The MIT Press.

The Future of Design Education in India. (2016, November). British Council.

The Sustainable Development Agenda. (n.d.). Retrieved 26 February 2019, from United Nations Sustainable Development website: https://www.un.org/sustainabledevelopment/development-agenda/.

Thomas, A. (2006). Design, Poverty, and Sustainable Development. *Design Issues*, *22*(4), 54–65.

Trivedi, K. (2003, February). Sarvodaya – Betterment of All. *ICSID News.*

Undergraduate Professional Programs -2019–20 | Srishti Institute of Art, Design and Technology. (n.d.). Retrieved 12 June 2023, from https://edge.dqlabs.in/colleges/srishti-manipal-institute-of-art-design-technology.

Vision & Mission: Industrial Design Centre (IDC) IIT Bombay, India. (n.d.). Retrieved 19 November 2018, from http://www.idc.iitb.ac.in/about/Vision_Mission.html.

Vision and Mission of MIT Group of Institutions, Pune. (n.d.). Retrieved 19 November 2018, from http://mitpune.ac.in/about-us/vision-mission.html.

Vision First – Proposal. (2011, February 11). Retrieved from https://visionpehle.wordpress.com/proposal/.

Ward, B. (1966). Spaceship Earth. New York: Columbia University Press.

What Is NVivo? | QSR International. (n.d.). Retrieved 5 March 2017, from http://www.qsrinternational.com/what-is-nvivo.

White, L., Jr. (1967). The Historical Roots of Our Ecologic Crisis. *Science*, *155*(3767), 1203–1207.

Whiteley, N. (1994). *Design for Society.* London: Reaktion Books, p. 16.

Wintle, C. (2017). Diplomacy and the Design School: The Ford Foundation and India's National Institute of Design. *Design and Culture*, *9*(2), 207–224. https://doi.org/10.1080/17547075.2017.1322876.

Index

Note: *Italic* page numbers refer to figures and page numbers followed by "n" denote endnotes.

For Product Safety Concerns and Information please contact our EU
representative GPSR@taylorandfrancis.com
Taylor & Francis Verlag GmbH, Kaufingerstraße 24, 80331 München, Germany

www.ingramcontent.com/pod-product-compliance
Lightning Source LLC
Chambersburg PA
CBHW051751230426
43670CB00012B/2235

* 9 7 8 1 0 3 2 4 6 8 0 2 0 *